What people are saying...

Courage for the Discouraged

"This is at heart a book of help and a book of hope.
In a season of great uncertainty and anxiety, it speaks very
practically, with honesty and insight. Simon's confidence in God's
commitment to bring us through the challenges and struggles we
all face is infectious. He encourages a way forward – rooted in the
promises of God's Word and a fresh rhythm of personal prayer – to
live a deeper and renewed life in daily relationship with Christ."

––––––

Chris Cartwright, General Superintendent. Elim churches

"Simon Lawton's book helps us see that it's not over until God says
so, and as long as there is breath in our lungs there is hope. *Courage
for the Discouraged* wasn't just written by Simon's pen and ink
though; it's been forged in the crucible of his own story. The
hammer of hardships has hit the anvil of his life in so many ways.
Yet every time he has gone through a trial, Simon has allowed God
to use it. This is a book that will help those of us who know that
our lives aren't perfect, and that God's plans can sometimes feel
confusing, to see that God is always at work in our lives. Simon
reminds us that we don't need to *understand* God to *trust* him, and
that in the end God wins."

––––––

**Malcolm Duncan,
pastor, author, theologian, broadcaster, FRSA**

"This book is like balm for the weary soul. Every section soothes the discouragement of the day and dispenses the medicinal power of hope where you need it most. I have no doubt that many people will be blessed and encouraged, both spiritually and emotionally, as they read Simon's honest and helpful words."

———

Cathy Madavan,
speaker, broadcaster and author of *Irrepressible: 12 Principles*
for a Courageous, Resilient and Fulfilling Life

"Displaying humility and transparency,
and writing with the heart of a true pastor, Simon Lawton has written a series of powerful encouragements that speak to an array of problems and disappointments we all may face in life. Using stories, scriptures and crafted prayers, Simon reveals a pathway through seasons of discouragement into a more blessed future. I highly recommend this book to all."

———

David Peters, director at Spiritlife Ministries in Auckland

"*Courage for the Discouraged* is filled with bite-sized devotionals that carry large-scale impact. If you find yourself in a season of frustration, disillusionment, uncertainty, or even angry at God, then this book is an excellent tool to realign you to his truth.
Filled with grace, saturated with scripture, and infused with the author's testimony, you will find someone who has navigated challenging seasons himself and yet come out the other side with wisdom and tools to help others walk freely. If you need a dose of courage today, read this book!"

———

Jen Baker, author and speaker

"Those who have read Simon Lawton's first book, *Imagine*, will not be disappointed by *Courage for the Discouraged*. Biblical, inspirational and practical, Simon has packed years of pastoral and personal experience into this volume, and all to good effect. Read it as a daily devotional, a personal spiritual development handbook, or, if you preach regularly, as something to spark your preaching imagination. Or just read it for a bit of encouragement. It works on all those levels."

––––

Pastor James Glass,
Elim regional leader, Scotland and Northwest England

"How do we gain courage when discouraged? For those facing discouragement, a wealth of insight is available from the truths contained within this book. Simon skillfully shows that courage comes from doing the right thing at the right time.

He shares biblical understanding that will help with the process of dealing with the discouragement that often arises from difficult life situations. I feel sure that the practical principles gained from his personal experience will equip readers in this challenging area, both now and in the future."

––––

Pastor Stephen Derbyshire,
City Gates Church, Ilford, London

COURAGE FOR THE

Discouraged

**Steps to restoring faith,
hope and strength**

Acknowledgments
Scripture quotations are primarily taken from the Holy Bible, New International Version Anglicised. Copyright Ó 1979, 1984, 2011 Biblica, formerly International Bible Society. Used by permission of Hodder & Stoughton Ltd, an Hachette UK company. All rights reserved. "NIV" is a registered trademark of Biblica. UK trademark number 1448790.

Scripture quotations marked (MSG) are taken from The Message. Copyright © 1993, 1994, 1995, 1996, 2000, 2001, 2002. Used by permission of NavPress Publishing Group.

Scripture quotations marked (NKJV) are taken from the New King James Version®. Copyright © 1982 by Thomas Nelson. Used by permission. All rights reserved.

Scripture quotations marked (NLT) are taken from the Holy Bible, New Living Translation, copyright © 1996, 2004, 2007, 2013, 2015 by Tyndale House Foundation. Used by permission of Tyndale House Publishers, Inc., Carol Stream, Illinois 60188. All rights reserved.

Scripture quotations marked (NASB) are taken from the New American Standard Bible®, Copyright © 1960,1962,1963,1968,1971,1972,1973,1975 ,1977,1995 by The Lockman Foundation. Used by permission.

A catalogue record for this book is available from the British Library

To Julia,

for sharing this incredible journey of life and ministry. You have made incredible sacrifices to follow the call of God with me. There have been many moments of incredible joy and fulfilment, yet also times of sadness, discouragement and despair. We have shared all the joys and heartaches together. You know and have lived every chapter in this book, as it's part of our story.

Thank you, Jules, for being you, and for being my soulmate on this incredible journey called life.

I couldn't have done it without you x

"Two are better than one, because they have a good return for their labour: if either of them falls down, one can help the other up. But pity anyone who falls and has no one to help them up. Also, if two lie down together, they will keep warm. But how can one keep warm alone? Though one may be overpowered, two can defend themselves. A cord of three strands is not quickly broken"
(Ecclesiastes 4:9-12).

CONTENTS

INTRODUCTION

The 'five deadly Ds' – discouragement, disappointment, disillusionment, despondency and despair – are all very real. I came to the conclusion prior to writing this book that every one of us experiences these feelings from time to time, and some of us are affected by them more regularly.

Pastors and Christian leaders are not exempt from this. One of the reasons for writing this book was that I have fought my own battles in these areas at times over the past few years. Some will be surprised to read this, others less so. These battles have been very real, and at times quite debilitating. I have lost entire mornings (thankfully not days) on several occasions, brought down by the battles raging in my mind and thoughts that have overwhelmed me.

Where do these feelings come from? I guess some are the natural outcomes of life's pressures, frustrations and disappointments, while others perhaps find their roots in mental health issues. However, I also believe that the enemy of our souls "prowls around like a roaring lion looking for someone to devour" (see 1 Peter 5:8). He seeks to steal, kill and destroy, and I strongly suspect that this starts with our thinking. Thankfully, our God is stronger, more powerful and, most significantly, on our side.

As we will discover, we are in good company. Charles Spurgeon, known as the 'prince of preachers' was a highly influential pastor and preacher in the 1800s, yet he reportedly said that he would not wish the depths of despair and discouragement he often experienced for long periods on his worst enemy.

Even the late, great evangelist Billy Graham faced similar challenges:

> "We may face even stronger temptations once we give our lives to Christ because Satan will do everything he can to discourage us and cause us to doubt our salvation. Remember: Satan's chief goal is to attack God in every way he possibly can – and one way he does that is by tempting believers to sin or become discouraged… [Satan] never gives up the fight."[1]

Billy made it clear that being a Christian was never going to be plain sailing and admitted that he experienced times of great discouragement himself. At these times he would pray to the Lord, often tearfully, and ask for God's help or forgiveness.

In 1841, Abraham Lincoln wrote to a law partner; "I am now the most miserable man living. If what I feel were equally distributed to the whole human family, there would not be one cheerful face on the earth."[2]

The Bible is also full of men and women who struggled with discouragement and despair, for example Elijah, Joshua and David, whom we will explore in detail later.

So how do we combat those dark days? Where do we go when we are feeling discouraged and need to discover fresh courage? How do we find renewed strength and hope in the face of disappointment, pain, loss, grief, challenge or trial?

I would suggest that the Word of God, which is powerful and life-giving, is the best starting point. For that reason, I've put together thirty days of thoughts and prayers (some from my own prayer journal) that I hope will encourage, strengthen and lift your head on those days when the five deadly Ds come at you in full force.

Let's never forget the incredible potential each of us has in Christ. The potential you, yes *you*, have in Christ. He thought you and I were worth creating. He obviously had a plan and chose to involve us in it.

> "It's in Christ that we find out who we are and what we are living for. Long before we first heard of Christ and got our hopes up, he had his eye on us, had designs on us for glorious living, part of the overall purpose he is working out in everything and everyone" (Ephesians 1:11-12, MSG).

Let's be people who reflect on His Word, pray and refuse to dwell in the dark place where the enemy longs for us to stay. Let's step out into His glorious light and choose to live in all that He has for us each day.

> "Your word is a lamp to guide my feet and a light for my path" (Psalm 119:105, NLT).

My prayer is that each person who reads this book will be inspired to focus on God and recultivate their relationship with Him, allowing Him to minister deeply into their souls. I pray that these thoughts will bring life, hope, restoration and renewed courage to all who find themselves in a season of discouragement and challenge.

God bless you!

Simon

Chapter 1

SHAKING OFF THE DARK CLOUDS

One of my favourite places on earth is a beautiful expanse of coastline called Benllech Bay on the island of Anglesey, North Wales. The views from the headland are spectacular, stretching across the magnificent golden sands toward Red Wharf Bay and beyond to the majestic mountains and peaks of Snowdonia.

Known as the sunshine island, a sea mist sometimes shrouds Anglesey for several days at a time, even during the summer. When this happens you can't see very far, and you certainly can't make out the mainland. However, if you were to drive off the island you would soon find yourself in bright sunshine, looking back at the island still shrouded in damp grey cloud. Those spectacular views are lost in the sea mist. On their first trip to the island, visitors would have no idea of the picturesque scenery lying just beyond their line of sight.

My life has been truly blessed, and I have enjoyed so many remarkable seasons and wonderful experiences, but I have to be honest and admit that there have also been seasons that were shrouded in dark, gloomy clouds. There are five dark clouds (or 'the five Ds', as I like to call them): disappointment, despondency, disillusionment, discouragement and despair. It's interesting that weather forecasters also use the term 'a depression' to describe a period of poor and unstable weather.

These clouds denote dark times. Often they occur without warning and become our dwelling place for too long. I know how it feels to stay in that place. Just like the outstanding natural scenery at Benllech Bay, the most awe-inspiring views can be lost when we become enveloped in those dark clouds. I've had to learn the importance of making the Lord my dwelling place when I find myself dwelling in the wrong places. It's not where God wants us to spend our time.

I must add at this juncture that I fully appreciate the massive difference between feeling down and clinical depression. My heart truly goes out to those suffering from the latter, and while my hope is that this book will in some way provide hope and encouragement to anyone going through the mill right now, those whose lives are impacted by stress, anxiety or depression may need to seek medical advice or to speak to a counsellor or trusted friend.

A prayer of Moses, who had vast and lengthy life experience, is quoted in Psalm 90. He declares:

> "Lord, you have been our dwelling-place throughout all generations" (Psalm 90:1).

The following psalm also encourages us to make God our dwelling place:

> "If you say, 'The Lord is my refuge,' and you make the Most High your dwelling, no harm will overtake you, no disaster will come near your tent. For he will command his angels concerning you to guard you in all your ways" (Psalm 91:9-11).

Don't dwell in the wrong places

Many of us have a tendency to find ourselves dwelling in the wrong places. As a teenager I was forever getting into trouble for being in the wrong place with the wrong people. During one summer camp in Benllech my friends and I decided to visit an old wreck in the middle of Red Wharf Bay. We had been repeatedly warned by the camp leaders not to walk across the bay because it became sinking sand when the tide turned and people could easily drown there.

The wreck was much further out than we had anticipated; however, after walking for some time we eventually reached it in the middle of the large bay. It was little more than a shell of sea-worn timbers, but we were overjoyed at our achievement.

As we turned around, a local fisherman appeared quite out of nowhere and warned us sternly that we were in grave danger, as the tide had turned. He told us to follow him back along the only safe path back to the beach, which we gratefully did. I still believe he was an angel in disguise who saved our lives.

Today, as a pastor, I would encourage you to dwell in the right places. Don't visit or remain too long in those negative places where the enemy wants you to stay. It's so easy to become discouraged, but that's just where he wants us in order to ruin our lives and to stop us experiencing and becoming everything God has called us to be.

Making your escape

> "Throughout their lives, they live under a cloud – frustrated, discouraged, and angry" (Ecclesiastes 5:17, NLT).

How can we escape these dark clouds? How can we move them along? I remember doing an open-air outreach event at a school fair in Leicestershire years ago. UK weather can be quite unpredictable, but we were delighted to find the day dry, warm and sunny. However, just before we were about to go on stage to share the gospel, dark black clouds began to head in our direction. We really prayed that God would change the wind direction and move them away, and that's exactly what happened. Amazing! In the Bible, Joshua prayed for the sun to stand still (see Joshua 10:12-13), so I guess we were in good company!

I believe it's possible to move the dark clouds in a natural and spiritual sense, but how do we do it? Paul speaks of this in 1 Corinthians 15:46 (NKJV):

> "However, the spiritual is not first, but the natural, and afterward the spiritual."

On occasion, God will demonstrate what he is able to do in the natural world prior to doing something incredible in the spiritual world. Whatever He can do for us naturally He can also do for us spiritually. While He can move the dark clouds away from a school fete, He can also take us from a place of discouragement and despair to a place of unexplained peace and hope.

First, we must make a choice not to dwell under these dark clouds and to push them away by dwelling in the right place – God's presence – instead. After all, He has promised that His presence will go with us wherever we are.

I find that praise, worship and thanksgiving remove the clouds and take me into His presence. Perhaps you need to spend more time being thankful for what you have rather than what you don't have. We can so easily forget all that God has blessed us with.

Why not take an inventory – not just counting what you have right now, but taking a trip down memory lane? With the help of the Holy Spirit, remember all that God has provided; all that He has blessed you with; all the miracles, large and small; all the provision, healing and deliverance. How short our memories are at times. He is a good, good father.

Second, I believe it is sometimes the enemy who sends these dark clouds of disappointment, disillusionment, despondency, discouragement and despair. When my wife Julia and I lived in Newcastle we weren't far from the coast, and occasionally on a beautiful summer's day the weather would change without any warning. The locals referred to it as a 'sea fret' when a cold, misty, low-level cloud would come in off the sea from nowhere, ruining the beautiful day.

I believe the enemy of our souls will attack our minds with those five dark clouds from time to time. It's horrible when it happens, and it comes out of nowhere. One minute the sun is shining and we're feeling fine, then suddenly we're under a deep cloud of oppression. Dark. Heavy. Horrible. The only way to deal with this kind of attack is to pray, asking God to remove those clouds.

Can I encourage you to recognise what is happening at times like this and pray? Sometimes as Christians we can be too passive. James urges us to "resist the devil, and he will flee from you" (see James 4:7).

Make a choice today that, with God's help, you will not allow the five Ds to shroud your life, but rather you will dwell in the light of His glory and presence.

Here's a prayer from my journal that I found myself praying one morning. Perhaps you could pray it over your life and situation. If necessary, pray it every day until you no longer need to, and of course feel free to adapt it and make it your own.

Father,

I will not allow my mind to be controlled by disappointment, despondency, disillusionment, discouragement or despair. I declare the truth of scripture, which says that I have the mind of Christ[3]. I break the stronghold of fear, anxiety and discouragement over my life. I command the dark clouds to depart in the name of Jesus, and I welcome the light of Your glory and presence into my life.

I will stop focusing on my disappointments, fears, weaknesses, inabilities, sinfulness and lack, and will start focusing on what I have inherited in Christ: a glorious strength, grace, power, provision and potency from heaven. His might, His power, His authority and His anointing is running through my spiritual veins.

I am Your child, whom You love, and I have been called for a purpose! Help me to focus on everything You are, to be thankful for everything I have, and to be everything You have called me to be in this season.

Amen

Further reading

Psalms 90 and 91.

Chapter 2

UNFORGOTTEN

I love a good crime drama or murder mystery. There is a TV crime drama series that runs every couple of years in the UK entitled *Unforgotten*, which deals with cold murder cases. A body will turn up on a building site or in a woodland area after someone has been missing for several decades, and the police begin reinvestigating the murder.

Because the police stopped investigating the person's disappearance years earlier, the family feels as though the deceased has been forgotten. They are, in fact, 'the unforgotten', hence the title of the show. 'Unforgotten' means 'not forgotten'. When someone dies we might say that they are 'gone but not forgotten'.

It's easy to believe at times that we have been forgotten by God. Below are some of the reasons why:

- You feel completely abandoned, ignored and uncared for by family, friends or even God. You may feel despised and rejected, or insignificant to the point that nobody even notices you.

- Your prayers don't appear to be answered as you anticipated, or maybe God seems to be silent.

- Your team leader, boss or pastor has overlooked you for a new role or promotion.

- You feel as though you've worked really hard and made tremendous sacrifices without any reward.

- Your expectations or dreams are currently unrealised.

There have been times over the years that I have experienced some of those feelings, but I've learned to trust God, obey Him and do whatever I can do to the best of my ability. And remember that if you're feeling insignificant or rejected, you're in good company:

> "[Jesus] was despised and rejected by mankind, a man of suffering, and familiar with pain. Like one from whom people hide their faces he was despised, and we held him in low esteem" (Isaiah 53:3).

God hasn't forgotten you

The truth is that God hasn't forgotten you, and He loves you. I'm sure there are lots of others who do as well, but maybe you're simply not aware of it.

I was walking my dog one evening and praying, and I was feeling really discouraged. I said to God: "Father, I need some encouragement right now. I feel discouraged about so many things." Almost immediately I looked down and saw a £1 coin glinting in the evening sunlight. I had to smile, as it was a small sign that God had not forgotten me. I have to be honest and say that a £20 note would have had a greater impact, but hey, beggars can't be choosers! Sometimes we can miss these small signs God gives us. What might you have missed lately?

I found myself praying and declaring all the challenges, issues, struggles, visions, desires, dreams and longings of my heart aloud. Concerning each one, I said: "Thank you, God, that you haven't forgotten."

Above all else, I remembered that He has promised never to leave or abandon me. That He is faithful and true. Isn't it amazing how, through simply finding a £1 coin, God was able to turn despair and discouragement into renewed hope and faith?

David felt forgotten

There were many times when King David must have felt forgotten. He experienced some amazing high points during his life: killing Goliath, uniting Judea and Israel as king, conquering the surrounding nations, and making Jerusalem the state capital.

However, there were also many low points, such as Saul's countless attempts to capture and kill him, hiding in caves (even after Samuel had anointed him as king!), living among the Philistines, his son Absalom's conspiracy against him, the murder of loyal friends and the death of his best friend Jonathan, his adultery with Bathsheba, the murder of Uriah and the loss of his unborn son.

I love the way the psalms record the raw honesty, humility and transparency of David. They remind me that it's OK not to be OK. It's not unusual to feel discouraged, frustrated, anxious and fearful at times. It's fine to wonder where God is and whether He has forgotten you.

Here are a couple of examples of David at his lowest ebb before his God:

"I am forgotten as though I were dead; I have become like broken pottery" (Psalm 31:12).

"Do not abandon me, O Lord. Do not stand at a distance, my God. Come quickly to help me, O Lord my savior" (Psalm 38:21-22, NLT).

Pour out your heart

At those low points when we feel forgotten, King David encourages us to trust in God and pour out our hearts to Him:

> "Trust in him at all times, you people; pour out your hearts to him, for God is our refuge" (Psalm 62:8).

Isn't that what David did in so many of his psalms? You might be surprised to discover that if you pour out your heart to God – whether you are angry, sad, fearful, discouraged, despondent or dissatisfied – that the Holy Spirit will, if you allow Him to, turn it into prayer and transition you into declaring God's truth and promises. I find this happens all the time. As I pour out what is inside me, the discouragement and despair turns into faith, hope and renewed courage, just as David's so often did:

"How long, Lord? Will you forget me for ever? How long will you hide your face from me? How long must I wrestle with my thoughts and day after day have sorrow in my heart? How long will my enemy triumph over me? Look on me and answer, Lord my God. Give light to my eyes, or I will sleep in death, and my enemy will say, 'I have overcome him,' and my foes will rejoice when I fall. But I trust in your unfailing love; my heart rejoices in your salvation. I will sing the Lord's praise, for he has been good to me" (Psalm 13:1-6).

David began by feeling forgotten ("Will you forget me for ever? How long will you hide your face from me?") but ended in faith and thanksgiving ("But I trust in your unfailing love... I will sing the Lord's praise...").

As we pour out our hearts, prayers and laments, a transaction occurs. We come to God with our fear, anxiety, frustration and concern, and leave with renewed hope through His wonderful truth and promises. Thank God for the Holy Spirit, who helps us in all our troubles.

We may feel as though we're forgotten at times, but God reminds us we're not. He never forgets us! I guess there are some things we should guard against if we're feeling forgotten. I've listed some below:

- Holding a grudge against those who appear to have forgotten about or rejected you.

- Losing interest in praying and reading the Bible.

- No longer attending church because you don't feel as though you are part of it any longer.

- Keeping everyone at arm's length.

- Allowing doubt, fear and anxiety to fill your heart.

- Permitting clouds of gloom, despondency and despair to take over your life. Refuse to sit under them!

- Listening to toxic voices or lies of the enemy.

- Indulging in any negative self-talk.

- Focusing on all that God *isn't doing* rather than all that He *has done* in the past or all that He *will do* in the future.

Can I encourage you to guard against those things and know that God is still God? He hasn't changed who He is, and He hasn't changed what He feels about you. You are His child and He will never forget you.

You are not forgotten by God!

I hope the following verses remind and encourage you that your Heavenly Father has not forgotten you. In fact, whenever you feel unloved, uncared for and unwanted, remember to whom you belong. You are not forgotten.

> "Can a mother forget the baby at her breast and have no compassion on the child she has borne? Though she may forget, I will not forget you!" (Isaiah 49:15).

"...For God has said, "I will never fail you. I will never abandon you"" (Hebrews 13:5, NLT).

"But God will never forget the needy; the hope of the afflicted will never perish" (Psalm 9:18).

So can I encourage you with this today? Next time you look at a pound coin or a dollar note, remember that God has not forgotten you!

Father,

I'm feeling a bit forgotten. Where are You? I pour out my heart to You today. I bring before You all the things that have made me feel forgotten and thank You that in all the areas of my life I'm concerned about [list them] You have not forgotten me. You see me and my situation.

Help me to trust You deeply, in spite of the circumstances that surround me. I choose to take part in a holy transaction, whereby discouragement, despair, anxiety and fear are replaced with faith, hope, renewed joy and an expectation of better days ahead.

Thank You that You will never leave nor forget me.

You are my faithful Father.

Amen

Further reading
Psalms 22, 27 and 142.

Chapter 3

YOU ARE NOT ON YOUR OWN

One of the most memorable photos of a US president was taken by reporter George Tames in 1961.[4] The picture poignantly shows John F. Kennedy standing hunched over his desk in the Oval Office reading the morning papers. He appears to be carrying the weight of the world on his shoulders, which he pretty much was. *The New York Times* later christened the photo "The Loneliest Job".

This reminds me of a guy in the Old Testament who felt very alone. He had done his best to stand up for righteousness and God's law, and had experienced a massive victory in defeating the prophets of Baal. However, Elijah not only felt as though God had completely deserted him after he'd defeated a fearsome enemy, but he also was living in fear for his life.

> "He replied, 'I have been very zealous for the Lord God Almighty. The Israelites have rejected your covenant, torn down your altars, and put your prophets to death with the sword. I am the only one left, and now they are trying to kill me too'" (1 Kings 19:10).

This wasn't the first time Elijah had felt alone, or that he was the only one standing up for righteousness:

> "Then Elijah said to them, 'I am the only one of the Lord's prophets left, but Baal has four hundred and fifty prophets'" (1 Kings 18:22).

The pitfalls of success

Discouragement often follows great success, and discouragement can lead to isolation. Whether we have experienced success or not, it's easy to feel as though we're on our own sometimes. Any lengthy period of challenge, trial or suffering can also lead us to believe we have been abandoned, and that perhaps God has forsaken us.

One of the greatest temptations during these periods is to become discouraged, disillusioned and despondent. These emotions can lead us to do the one thing we should never do: withdraw from fellowship and the much-needed encouragement and support of others.

"*Solitude* is a gift from God. Isolation is not – it's a tool of the Enemy" (Carey Nieuwhof).[5]

With God's help, Elijah had achieved an incredible victory over the prophets of Baal (see 1 Kings 18:19-40). He challenged King Ahab to gather them all on top of Mount Carmel before the whole nation to prove which was the true God. The altars were built and the sacrifices were laid on them, then Elijah told the people that the true God would be the one who sent fire down to consume the sacrifice. We know from the narrative that Jehovah (the one true God) showed up and consumed everything, and as a result the prophets of Baal were slaughtered. It was an outstanding miracle.

Elijah demonstrated outstanding faith and trust in God when his life was under immediate threat. Imagine if the fire hadn't fallen. I'm not sure I would have trusted God enough or had the faith to do what he did. However, God sometimes calls us to trust Him, step out into challenging situations and do great exploits for Him.

Elijah achieved a spectacular victory against Ahab and the Prophets of Baal. So often when we accomplish something great for God there is a retaliatory attack from the enemy of our souls. He rarely allows us the opportunity to relax. This is why Peter warns us to:

> "Stay alert! Watch out for your great enemy, the devil. He prowls around like a roaring lion, looking for someone to devour" (1 Peter 5:8, NLT).

The loneliness of leadership

Elijah must have gone from being the most popular guy in Israel to being very, very alone. Thanks to Jezebel's death threats he became a fugitive on the run, living in fear of his life. Why? Because as a leader he did the right thing and stood up for righteousness. He refused to tolerate evil. Leadership can be a lonely place at times.

Some reading this will be in leadership in the workplace, church community or at home. The nature of leadership is that you are the one who has to make the tough calls, stand up for what is right, bring correction and lead others forward. Whether you are successful or not, there is often great loneliness for those who lead. To any disheartened leaders reading, I would encourage you with the verses below.

> "Think how you have instructed many, how you have strengthened feeble hands. Your words have supported those who stumbled; you have strengthened faltering knees. But now trouble comes to you, and you are discouraged; it strikes you, and you are dismayed" (Job 4:3-5).

But the Lord says to you:

> "I took you from the ends of the earth, from its farthest corners I called you. I said, 'You are my servant'; I have chosen you and have not rejected you. So do not fear, for I am with you; do not be dismayed, for I am your God. I will strengthen you and help you; I will uphold you with my righteous right hand" (Isaiah 41:9-10).

Whether you are a leader or not, we all experience wilderness seasons where we feel like we're on our own. We can feel as though it's us versus the world at times. I've experienced periods when it felt as though God had gone completely AWOL; times when I couldn't sense His presence and I felt as though my prayers were hitting the ceiling. All I could say was: "Where are you, Lord?"

But no matter whether we can feel God's presence or not, He remains faithful and is always with us. He will never leave or abandon us.

Joshua's courage

No book on courage would be complete without mentioning Joshua (to whom we will return later):

> "Then Moses summoned Joshua and said to him in the presence of all Israel, 'Be strong and courageous, for you must go with this people into the land that the Lord swore to their ancestors to give them, and you must divide it among them as their inheritance. The Lord himself goes before you and will be with you; he will never leave you nor forsake you. Do not be afraid; do not be discouraged'" (Deuteronomy 31:7-8).

God repeatedly promised Joshua that He would go before and be with him, and also that Joshua would conquer the Promised Land.

He knew Joshua would become doubtful, discouraged and fearful at times, and the same applies to you and me.

An example of this is found in Joshua 7 when Achan sinned by taking items that had been devoted to God from Jericho for himself. The children of Israel had obeyed God and completely destroyed Jericho, moving on to attack Ai, which should have been a straightforward battle. However, they were surprisingly routed by the men of Ai. The narrative tells us that the people were fearful and that Joshua tore his clothes and fell face down before the Lord until evening, questioning why God had brought the people across the River Jordan. This was a moment when I'm sure Joshua must have felt discouraged and fearful. But God revealed to him the sin that had occurred within the camp and gave him a strategy to deal with it.

No matter what we face each day, our role is to trust God deeply like Joshua. We need to seek His face and depend on His strength to help and support us on the journey. We may feel afraid sometimes, but we are never alone.

"God is always near us. Always for us. Always in us" (Max Lucado).[6]

As the saying goes: "Leadership is certainly not a popularity contest." Everyone will be looking for you to lead in these situations. There will, on occasion, be opposition, intimidation and even confrontation. I'm sure Joshua must have experienced all of these issues when he publicly dealt with Achan's sin.

So take courage today. The God of Abraham, Isaac and Jacob is with you. The God of Elijah and Joshua is with you. The Lord of heaven's armies is with you. Trust Him deeply and know that you are not alone. He is with you.

Father,

I realise I'm in good company today. Two giants of the Old Testament, Elijah and Joshua, also had issues with fear, discouragement and loneliness. Help me to be strong, full of wisdom and courage, and totally dependent on You as I follow the path You have laid out for me. Thank You that You are with me, that You go before me and that I will achieve the purposes You have placed me on Planet Earth to fulfil. Help me to keep my eyes fixed on You, today and every day.

Amen

Further reading

Psalm 139; Psalm 23:4; Romans 8:38-39.

Chapter 4

DON'T LOSE HOPE IN THE STORM

I've watched videos that people have shared on social media of cruise liners being battered at sea by enormous waves. It's not an experience I would enjoy! I think my worst experience of being in a storm at sea was taking the ferry across the English Channel from Dover to Dunkirk; a mere thirty-eight nautical miles. I felt really sick for the entire crossing, and it didn't help when someone later informed me that it had just been a mild swell.

Paul and his fellow passengers experienced a severe storm that lasted many days during their journey to Rome. I can't imagine what it must have been like. They tried everything they could to keep the ship afloat, even to the point of throwing cargo and the ship's tackle overboard, but still the situation didn't change. Many days in, and presumably having had little sleep and even less food and water, they must have been shattered, starving and really scared:

"When neither sun nor stars appeared for many days and the storm continued raging, we finally gave up all hope of being saved" (Acts 27:20).

There was only one conclusion to draw… they were doomed to go down with the ship! They had lost all hope of being rescued, and besides, there were no flares or radios to send out a Mayday, and certainly no coastguards or air-sea rescue to bail them out.

But Paul spoke into their situation and encouraged them, saying:

> "But now I urge you to keep up your courage, because not one of you will be lost; only the ship will be destroyed. Last night an angel of the God to whom I belong and whom I serve stood beside me and said, 'Do not be afraid, Paul. You must stand trial before Caesar; and God has graciously given you the lives of all who sail with you.' So keep up your courage, men, for I have faith in God that it will happen just as he told me" (Acts 27:22-25).

It's a massive challenge to stay courageous in the middle of a storm, especially when it feels as though there has been no daylight for weeks. The storm continues to rage and everything remains dark. You wonder when, or if, the sun will ever shine again.

Begin to hope again

I want to encourage you today to revert your focus to God and to begin to hope again. Our hope in Jesus Christ should be the anchor of our faith. Our hope is secure, in that we know who God is, and what Jesus has done and still does.

> "We have this hope as an anchor for the soul, firm and secure…" (Hebrews 6:19).

To hope is to understand His nature, character, faithfulness, love and mercy, and to trust Him completely. Hope is an assurance that our "times are in [His] hands" (see Psalm 31:15).

The sailors looked at the circumstances – the storm, the wind and the waves – and abandoned all hope because they forgot that God was in control. This is often our greatest weakness. When we're in the middle of a storm we can so easily become discouraged and quickly jump to the conclusion that God is no longer in control, cannot be trusted, doesn't care, or has forgotten us and will let us go. However, this is contrary to the truth and promises of scripture.

Often when nothing appears to be happening we become just like those sailors. We give up praying, believing and expecting God to act. Yet this is precisely the time to cling to God and pray! In spite of the fact that you cannot see anything changing, today is another day to press in, trust and believe. Another day to have hope!

How can I say all this? Because I've been in some pretty desperate situations and have seen God at work. I've been through dark days, when everything that could go wrong did go wrong, when the money had run out and the debts were overwhelming, when there was no food to put on the table and there were no presents for the children at Christmas.

I've experienced loss, bereavement, rejection, attacks, sleepless nights, pressure and even breakdown. Yet every single time, and without fail, God has sustained me and my family and has brought us through. In fact, we have seen God's miraculous provision and amazing breakthroughs on many occasions!

God is at work in the storm

Every one of those storms has been allowed by God to build assurance and strengthen our faith. They weren't pleasant at the time, but as I look back I thank God for what He built in me through those challenging times (see Romans 5:2-5).

Some of you are learning how to really trust God in the storm right now. Your faith is being challenged and stretched. It's not easy or fun, but the God of all hope is with you. During this season He is developing your character, strengthening your faith and increasing your confidence in Him.

> "Now faith is confidence in what we hope for and assurance about what we do not see. This is what the ancients were commended for" (Hebrews 11:1-2).

What are the attributes of hope?

Hope is not wishful thinking. It's based on our knowledge, understanding and experience of Father God. We have hope because of who He is. Hard as it may be, we must make a choice through the darkest, most difficult days to "live by faith not by sight" (see 2 Corinthians 5:7).

Hope says: "I will *not* quit!" Hope keeps going against all the odds. It perseveres no matter what obstacles, storms or people come against us. It says: "I've come this far and I'm not giving up now! I'm too close!"

"When you say a situation or a person is hopeless, you are slamming the door in the face of God" (Charles L. Allen).[7]

God told Abraham and Sarah they were going to have a baby at ninety and a hundred years old, respectively. Bear in mind that Sarah was also barren! But the rest is history. Paul reminds us that:

"Against all hope, Abraham in hope believed and so became the father of many nations, just as it had been said to him, 'So shall your offspring be'" (Romans 4:18).

I have stood on that verse so many times.

Abraham is a great example of the fact that hope gets God's attention. In fact, it's actually not that hard to get His attention because He's already looking:

"But the eyes of the Lord are on those who fear him, on those whose hope is in his unfailing love, to deliver them from death and keep them alive in famine. We wait in hope for the Lord; he is our help and our shield. In him our hearts rejoice, for we trust in his holy name. May your unfailing love be with us, Lord, even as we put our hope in you" (Psalm 33:18-22).

Hope attracts Him because it's a powerful expression of our faith. God isn't looking for doubters, moaners and groaners. He's looking for those who will demonstrate absolute faith in Him and not anyone else. He's looking for those who will wake up every morning feeling expectant; for those who will say, "Today's the day, Lord", and believe it!

Hope renews our strength in God. As Isaiah suggests below, even young people become weary and lose their strength, but God renews and strengthens those with little strength left:

"He gives strength to the weary and increases the power of the weak. Even youths grow tired and weary, and young men stumble and fall; but those who hope in the Lord will renew their strength. They will soar on wings like eagles; they will run and not grow weary, they will walk and not be faint" (Isaiah 40:29-31).

Hope anticipates, welcomes and expects what is sure. As Paul said to the guys who were struggling in the ship:

"So keep up your courage, men, for I have faith in God that it will happen just as he told me" (Acts 27:25).

Desmond Tutu said that:

"Hope is being able to see that there is light despite all of the darkness."[8]

Perhaps you're in a dark place or the middle of a storm today. If so, don't lose hope. Be expectant and keep your eyes on Jesus, who is the Light in the midst of your storm. He is the One who spoke to the storm the disciples found themselves in, and said: "Peace, be still!" (see Mark 4:39, NKJV). Suddenly the wind stopped and there was a great calm.

There is hope in the middle of your storm.

This is my prayer for you today, and perhaps you should pray it over your own situation:

"May the God of hope fill you with all joy and peace as you trust in him, so that you may overflow with hope by the power of the Holy Spirit" (Romans 15:13).

Further reading

Romans 5:1-5 and 8:18-39.

Chapter 5

GOD SEES

Several years ago we were doing some outreach on the streets of Newcastle, and as we walked around the city centre we prayerfully asked God whom we should approach. We ended up approaching three separate people. The first, a local guy, had been searching for God and had taken up reading his Bible a year earlier. The second, a young woman from New Zealand, had been studying the Bible with a friend and came to faith during our conversation. The third, a postgraduate from Nottingham who was just visiting for the weekend, also became a Christian at this point. It turned out her friend had been inviting her to church for weeks!

God sees! We shouldn't be surprised by events like this. I love the fact that Jesus had already seen Nathanael, who became one of the disciples, before they met:

> "'How do you know me?' Nathanael asked. Jesus answered, 'I saw you while you were still under the fig-tree before Philip called you'" (John 1:48).

God sees everything

I'm reassured by the fact that God sees everything. He is present everywhere, and in fact one of the Hebrew names for God is *El roi*, "the God who sees (me)". We should be encouraged that there is no circumstance that escapes his fatherly awareness and care.

Job understood God's omnipresence:

> "For he views the ends of the earth and sees everything under the heavens" (Job 28:24).

God knows us. He is aware of our troubles, thoughts and feelings. He sees when we are happy and when we are sad. He sees our joy and our discouragement. Jesus said that the hairs on our heads are numbered by God, and that he notices when a single sparrow falls to the ground (see Matthew 10:29-30; Luke 12:7). This tells us that God sees the circumstances of our lives in detail. It's amazing to think that He had His eye on us even before we knew Him.

> "It's in Christ that we find out who we are and what we are living for. Long before we first heard of Christ and got our hopes up, he had his eye on us, had designs on us for glorious living, part of the overall purpose he is working out in everything and everyone" (Ephesians 1:11-12, MSG).

He is the God who sees. But *what* does He see?

God sees our pain, struggles and suffering

After Abraham and Sarai's slave, Hagar, became pregnant with Abraham's son, Ishmael, she was treated so harshly by Sarai that she eventually ran away, escaping into the desert. The angel of the Lord found her there and told her to return to Abraham and Sarai, announcing that she would have many other children.

"[Hagar] gave this name to the Lord who spoke to her: 'You are the God who sees me,' for she said, "I have now seen the One who sees me"" (Genesis 16:13).

You may be feeling discouraged today and wondering where God is. Perhaps you feel alone in your struggles. Rest assured that God sees, hears and is close to the broken-hearted. He remains your strong deliverer, protector and provider (see Psalm 34:15-18). He is faithful.

God sees and knows our anxious thoughts

Psalm 139:1-23 tells us that He knows our every thought:

"You have searched me, Lord, and you know me. You know when I sit and when I rise; you perceive my thoughts from afar… Search me, God, and know my heart; test me and know my anxious thoughts."

God sees and hears. He is aware of how anxious we can become at times. He knows. He understands. He gets you. He doesn't condemn. –In fact, He has planned an escape route that works:

"Cast all your anxiety on him because he cares for you"
(1 Peter 5:7).

He actually wants you to unload that stuff onto Him. Yes, all of it. He has broad shoulders. After all, He is the One who said:

"Come to me, all you are weary and burdened, and I will give you rest" (Matthew 11:28).

Perhaps as you're reading this you think that sounds simplistic and twee; however, I have discovered that this works. Practise it each day, every time you become anxious and weary, and you will be surprised by the difference it makes. In fact, Jesus promised this would be the result:

'Take my yoke upon you and learn from me, for I am gentle and humble in heart, and you will find rest for your souls' (Matthew 11:29).

Make a choice today not to allow yourself to carry unnecessary anxiety but rather to find rest for your soul.

God sees what lies behind and what lies ahead

Our minds can be so clouded by the past that we sometimes fail to see the reality of the present and the potential of the future. You may have experienced terrible things. Perhaps you have been hurt, abused, rejected, humiliated, ignored or forgotten. God sees it all. He saw Hagar and heard her cry, and He also sees you. Perhaps it's time to start letting go of the past, to forgive and forget. Perhaps it's time to stop looking back and to begin moving forward.

"But forget all that—it is nothing compared to what I am going to do. For I am about to do something new. See, I have already begun! Do you not see it? I will make a pathway through the wilderness. I will create rivers in the dry wasteland" (Isaiah 43:18-19, NLT).

God sees and rewards what we do in secret

While no one else may notice, God sees what you do in secret and has promised to reward you (see Matthew 6:3-6). You may have been faithful in serving God, giving sacrificially and keeping your family together. You may also have paid the price in terms of tiredness or unpopularity. But it doesn't go unnoticed:

"God is not unjust; he will not forget your work and the love you have shown him as you have helped his people and continue to help them" (Hebrews 6:10).

Have you ever wondered whether anyone has noticed all that you do in serving Him and His people? Many of us have asked ourselves this question. The truth is, God sees it even if no one else does, and He will reward you for it.

God sees our weariness and desires to strengthen us

When we are fully committed to Him, it costs us, and it can be wearying. I've had three friends in pastoral ministry step down over the last few years because they were just worn out. It can happen to anyone.

> "For the eyes of the Lord range throughout the earth to strengthen those whose hearts are fully committed to him..." (2 Chronicles 16:9).

God sees our commitment to Him. He sees the price we pay at times, the challenges we face in being true followers of Christ and our unwillingness to compromise His Word. But His grace is sufficient for each one of us (see 2 Corinthians 12:9). He sees our dedication and tiredness, and He promises to strengthen us.

God sees things differently from us!

As a pastor, father and husband, I am constantly asking God for wisdom and insight. I long for greater revelation; to see things the way He sees them.

> "'For my thoughts are not your thoughts, neither are your ways my ways,' declares the Lord. 'As the heavens are higher than the earth, so are my ways higher than your ways and my thoughts than your thoughts'" (Isaiah 55:8-9).

He knows what's happening because, as He Himself declares:

> "I am the Alpha and the Omega, the First and the Last, the Beginning and the End" (Revelation 22:13).

We may find ourselves saying: "Dear God, I can't cope. This isn't fair. What's happening?" His response is: "It's OK, for I know the end from the beginning."

God sees! He knows the past, the present and the future. He knows the outcomes. He holds everything in His hands. We should trust that He knows best!

God watches over your life

> "He will not let your foot slip – he who watches over you will not slumber; indeed, he who watches over Israel will neither slumber nor sleep. The Lord watches over you – the Lord is your shade at your right hand; the sun will not harm you by day, nor the moon by night. The Lord will keep you from all harm – he will watch over your life; the Lord will watch over your coming and going both now and for evermore"
> (Psalm 121:3-8).

I personally find it incredibly reassuring to know that I have a Father who watches over me as I go out and come in; that He is constantly with me and watching over my life. He will never switch off for a moment because He is the God who actively watches over me. Five times the psalmist repeats this idea of God watching in the verses above.

Be encouraged today. The Lord sees and watches over you.

Father,

Thank You that You see me and watch over my life. You know everything about me. You know my every anxious thought (cast them onto Him now). You saw my first breath and You'll be there for my last. Thank You that You never switch off or take time out. You are always there. You are totally reliable. I place my life in Your hands again today. I know I can trust You to lead me. Strengthen me today, and help me not to be anxious about anything but to rest in You. Enable me to see as You see and think as you think.

Lord, give me Your eyes to see and notice, and Your ears to listen and hear. Let me use my lips to encourage, lift up, strengthen and bring hope to those who are struggling.

Amen

Further reading
Psalm 139:13-16.

Chapter 6

MORE THAN ENOUGH GRACE

Julia and I had a friend whose husband was lovely most of the time, but who could sometimes be very difficult. We would regularly ask her: "How do you cope with him?" Her reply, given with a smile on her face each time, was that she simply prayed for more grace every time he was difficult.

"But He gives us more grace..." (James 4:6).

When people and situations prove challenging it can become very discouraging. This feeling may increase if the issues multiply or continue for any length of time. Many of us have experienced periods in our lives where it feels as though everything and everyone is against us, and perhaps you are experiencing a time like this right now.

There have been occasions in my life when I have faced opposition from difficult people. Years ago, when we planted our first church, I remember working at the Royal Mail sorting office to earn some extra money at Christmas. I enjoyed the work and meeting new people; however, one lady constantly attacked me and was always in my face. She made my life hell at times. I needed plenty of grace and patience when she was around.

Perhaps someone in your world is making your life hell right now, and without good reason. Maybe a boss, work colleague, neighbour or even a friend or family member is making your life a misery. You may even dread answering the phone or opening your emails. I've been there, so I understand how disheartening and discouraging this can be. It's easy to become anxious and fearful in these situations. You can reach the point where you're constantly on edge, wondering what that person is going to say or do next.

The writer to the Hebrews encourages us to follow Jesus' example and keep our perspective:

> "…Let us run with perseverance the race marked out for us, fixing our eyes on Jesus, the pioneer and perfecter of faith. For the joy that was set before him he endured the cross, scorning its shame, and sat down at the right hand of the throne of God. Consider him who endured such opposition from sinners, so that you will not grow weary and lose heart" (Hebrews 12:1-3).

Consider Jesus

Jesus endured opposition and the cross in order to experience the joy of resurrection and the salvation of mankind. If you're feeling discouraged today, consider all that Jesus experienced. Then ask, just as our friend so often did, for more grace. I'm sure Jesus Himself requested more grace from His Father during those early mornings and quiet times away from the crowds. He didn't simply tolerate the demanding groups of people who followed him everywhere, the judgemental Pharisees or the often thoughtless and slow-on-the-uptake disciples. He actually found fresh grace each day to meet people where they were and to love, teach and care for them.

Thank God that – in the midst of all you are facing, in the midst of graceless, thoughtless people, and in the midst of discouraging circumstances – His Grace is sufficient for it all.

Paul had to remind Timothy, in all the challenges he faced leading the churches, to:

"…be strong in the grace that is in Christ Jesus" (2 Timothy 2:1).

His grace changes people

So don't lose heart. Keep going. I really prayed about the difficult lady at Royal Mail. She was awful to me and her tongue could cut me to pieces. It got to the point where I dreaded rest breaks. Then one day she sat next to me and confessed that she had been wrong to attack me. She wanted to know why I never retaliated and had such a peace about me. As you can imagine, I took the opportunity to share my faith with her and she attended our church for a short time.

That difficult person, that workmate who makes your life a misery or that challenging family member needs to be a recipient of God's amazing grace just as much as we do.

"For from his fullness we have all received, grace upon grace" (John 1:16, ESV).

The Bible tells us there is more than enough grace for me and for you, and that, just as He has shared His abundant grace with us, we also should share it with those in need:

"Be kind and compassionate to one another, forgiving each other, just as in Christ God forgave you" (Ephesians 4:32).

God blesses us with fresh grace and mercy every day. Let's make sure we are vessels of His grace for those whose paths we cross.

I wonder who your difficult person is. Who is making your life a misery? It could actually be a cry for help from deep within. See this situation as an opportunity to show grace to a troubled soul. Start praying for that person every day. You may be surprised by what God does in them and in you.

Prayer

Father,

Thank You that in everything I face, today and every day, Your grace is sufficient for me. I bring before You all the challenging people and difficult situations in my life [list them]. I ask for more grace, and I forgive all those who are making my life difficult right now. Father bless them. I choose to delight in my weaknesses in order that Your grace and incredible favour might rest upon me. In my weakness, I ask You to supply me with fresh enthusiasm, energy and strength for the life You have given me. Help me to be a blessing to others today in spite of everything I'm facing.

In Jesus' name,
Amen

Further reading

Hebrews 4:16; 2 Peter 1:2; James 4:6.

Chapter 7

FIND SOMEONE TO ENCOURAGE TODAY

I t doesn't matter who you are, where you've come from or what you've achieved in life, we all need encouragement. Alpha founder Nicky Gumbel tweeted:

"One of the best gifts you can give anyone is encouragement. If everyone received enough the world would blossom beyond our wildest dreams."[9]

The world can be a pretty discouraging place at times, and often people don't help! As pastor and leadership expert, John Maxwell, says:

"Remember, man does not live by bread alone; sometimes he needs a little buttering up."[10]

Encouragement isn't simply a great leadership principle, or a way of making friends and influencing people. It is also a command of scripture. The apostle Paul writes to the Thessalonian believers:

> "Therefore encourage one another and build each other up, just as in fact you are doing. Now we ask you, brothers and sisters, to acknowledge those who work hard among you, who care for you in the Lord and who admonish you. Hold them in the

highest regard in love because of their work. Live in peace with each other. And we urge you, brothers and sisters, warn those who are idle and disruptive, encourage the disheartened, help the weak, be patient with everyone. Make sure that nobody pays back wrong for wrong, but always strive to do what is good for each other and for everyone else" (1 Thessalonians 5:11-15).

The command to encourage one another is found numerous times in the New Testament, which emphasises its importance. In fact, the writer to the Hebrews suggests that we need encouragement every day:

> "But encourage one another daily, as long as it is called 'Today', so that none of you may be hardened by sin's deceitfulness" (Hebrews 3:13).

The tragedy is that we find it easier to criticise, judge and tear people down than to lift them up and generally be positive. What a different place our world would be if we took the time to simply encourage people.

"Be an encourager. The world has plenty of critics already" (Dave Willis).[11]

A ministry of encouragement

The devil has a ministry of discouragement, so we must counter this with a ministry of encouragement. Let's make sure we don't do his work for him, but rather that we provide an antidote to the world's negativity.

Barnabas was known as an encourager. Acts 4:36 records that his real name was Joseph, but the disciples called him Barnabas, which meant "son of encouragement". The original Greek word used is *paraklesis*, which means encouragement, consolation, comfort, exhortation and entreaty.

What actually happens when we encourage one another?

- We build people up, injecting life, strength, confidence, hope and joy into their lives.

- We refresh, renew and raise spirits.

- We energise and enthuse.

- We strengthen resolve.

- We inspire people to be more determined, daring, hopeful and confident, and more likely to achieve something great!

- We counter the negatives. Often the negative words spoken over people's lives and into their souls will lift as we counter them with positive words of encouragement.

Sometimes one person saying, "You know what? You can do this!" counters the person's negative thoughts, doubts, fears and anxieties. When we encourage others we actually help to release fresh courage in them. Confidence and belief return. They become invigorated. Can't becomes can, negatives become positives and a way is found where previously there was no way.

Change someone's life!

Imagine the difference it makes to someone who is feeling discouraged to receive a word of encouragement. Imagine the difference it makes to someone who is low on confidence, struggling with insecurity, feeling unappreciated or on the verge of quitting.

Can I also say this? Even super confident, successful people who seemingly have it all together need encouragement. Don't forget them as you encourage others. They may appear to be thriving, but everyone needs encouragement. We all need building up. We all need to hear encouraging, life-giving words. With a few encouraging words, you have the ability to change the course of someone's day, week or even their life.

In my study at home I have several cards that were given to me by members of the three congregations I have been privileged to serve over the years. Each card contains words of encouragement and appreciation of my ministry. During that same period, I have, on occasion, received discouraging letters. As you can imagine, I have retained none of these. On those low days we all experience, I sometimes read those positive cards and remind myself that, while I am by no means perfect, I'm not as bad as I or others may think. I'm encouraged and reinvigorated by the words of others each time.

An antidote for discouragement

On days when we find ourselves feeling particularly discouraged, I believe one of the best things we can do is choose to forget about our own circumstances and prayerfully consider others who might need our encouragement that day. Often we get encouragement from being an encourager. A simple word of encouragement could be like a drop of rain in a parched desert.

> "Worry weighs a person down; an encouraging word cheers a person up" (Proverbs 12:25, NLT).

A few years ago, when our son and his wife were visiting with one of our first grandchildren, I sensed that my daughter-in-law felt she wasn't doing a very good job as a first-time mother. I felt God say to me: "Encourage her."

As they turned to leave there were hugs all round. When I hugged my daughter-in-law, I whispered in her ear: "You're a great mum, you know." I could see from her response what this meant to her. I'm pretty sure those six words gave her a massive lift to know how appreciated she was, and that others had noticed she was a good mother.

No matter how discouraged you feel today, find someone else to encourage. You have the power to change someone's day with your encouragement. In fact, make a point of being an encourager to as many people as possible. Your words, which cost very little, could just change someone's life.

You may be wondering who in your circle needs encouragement right now. The simple answer is this: if they're breathing they will benefit from your encouragement.

So the question is this, who are you going to encourage today?

Father,

I know what it is to feel discouraged. It's a horrible, lonely place. Help me to step out of discouragement and into encouragement. Help me to see people with Your eyes and to spot those who particularly need encouraging words or a hug. Give me exactly the right words; words that will bring life, hope and blessing. May I be a channel of Your encouragement and blessing today.

In Jesus' name,
Amen

Further reading

Hebrews 10:24-25; 2 Corinthians 13:11; Ephesians 4:29; Luke 6:38.

Chapter 8

DON'T FOCUS ON THE WAVES

Julia and I recently spent a few days in a beautiful Caswell Bay apartment on the Gower peninsula. The area is classified as an area of outstanding natural beauty, and it certainly lives up to this description. Our apartment was in a stunning location just a few feet away from the sea, and every day we sat and watched the waves go in and out. What struck me was the relentlessness of the sea and the waves. Wave after wave headed towards the rocks, creating quite a spectacle as they relentlessly pounded the rocky shoreline.

Our lives can feel like they are being relentlessly pounded at times. It feels like one thing after another as wave upon wave hits us. There have been several seasons in my life where it has felt exactly like this, with financial difficulties, ill health, challenging people and untold pressures on every side. And just as you think the water has ebbed away and settled down another giant roller hits you!

> "Deep calls to deep in the roar of your waterfalls; all your waves and breakers have swept over me" (Psalms 42:7).

So how do we face these challenges?

Like many of us, Paul was tempted to give up at times. On one occasion he felt as though he had a death sentence hanging over him. He wrote this to the Corinthian believers:

> "We do not want you to be uninformed, brothers and sisters, about the troubles we experienced in the province of Asia. We were under great pressure, far beyond our ability to endure, so that we despaired of life itself. Indeed, we felt we had received the sentence of death. But this happened that we might not rely on ourselves but on God, who raises the dead. He has delivered us from such a deadly peril, and he will deliver us again. On him we have set our hope that he will continue to deliver us" (2 Corinthians 1:8-10).

This an amazing admission from the great apostle, and later in the same letter he offers a solution for times like this:

> "Therefore we do not lose heart. Though outwardly we are wasting away, yet inwardly we are being renewed day by day. For our light and momentary troubles are achieving for us an eternal glory that far outweighs them all. So we fix our eyes not on what is seen, but on what is unseen, since what is seen is temporary, but what is unseen is eternal" (2 Corinthians 4:16-18).

Don't lose heart

Many of the challenges you face are not unusual. Paul faced many of them himself. But remember that God is at work in your situation. He is working spiritual growth, maturity and renewal in you for His glory. He is the God who rescues, restores and redeems. The struggle will eventually stop. The waves will cease.

As Julia and I sat there each day, enjoying the stunning Welsh scenery and watching the awesome power of God and the relentlessness of the waves, a recurring story unfolded. Eventually the tide would turn, the waves would settle and a beautiful sandy beach would appear. We watched the golden sands become a hive of activity as families enjoyed life in the sunshine, couples walked their dogs and children played in the rock pools.

Get your focus right

My prayer for you is that rather than focusing on the wind and waves you will focus on God and what is, as yet, unseen. God is always at work behind the scenes. The problem is, we can't always see what He is working on while we're going through the storm. Yet be sure that He is working to turn things around for your good, and that one day you will see what He has been preparing for you or preparing *you* for.

> "That is what the Scriptures mean when they say, 'No eye has seen, no ear has heard, and no mind has imagined what God has prepared for those who love him'" (1 Corinthians 2:9, NLT).

It's so easy to lose sight of God in times of deep discouragement and despair. To forget that He is the rock of ages; the One who is faithful and true. Instead, we are tempted to focus on what we can see; the very things that have caused us to despair in the first place.

The question is this: what will you choose to focus on? You can either focus on your troubles and challenges or on the unseen One. In my experience, the more I focus on the areas of my life that are bringing me discouragement and despair the worse they look and the more discouraged I become. I can easily lose perspective, so it's critical that I focus on God and allow my life to be flooded once again with waves of His power, presence, glory and goodness. As I do that I'm reminded of His faithfulness, His unchanging nature and His love and care for me. I realise He hasn't forgotten me and that I can fully entrust my present and my future to His dependable care.

Boot camp

As I focus on God, I'm also reminded that He is the author and perfecter of my faith (Hebrews 12:2), and I become aware that there may well be some authoring and perfecting taking place. God turns what the enemy intends for harm on its head to mould, shape and equip us for all that He has planned for our lives.

He wants us to be well prepared. The Royal Marines go through all kinds of hell to prepare them for the service that lies ahead. It is not a holiday camp or a luxury cruise, but rather a place of preparation for elite troops who will one day be fighting for Queen and country!

So while we continue to undergo God's preparation course, let's keep our focus on Him and not on the waves. David makes the same declaration twice in Psalm 42:

> "Why, my soul, are you downcast? Why so disturbed within me? Put your hope in God, for I will yet praise him, my Saviour and my God" (Psalm 42:5 and 11).

I believe that the tide is turning and that better days than you are currently experiencing lie ahead. I'm believing that some of the things God has been working on without your knowledge will soon be released into your situation. He is full of surprises.

Father,

I'm struggling right now. It seems as though my life is being hit by wave upon wave, and I'm finding it hard to keep my head above water. I'm doing my best to trust You in the midst of the storm and to believe that better days lie ahead. I choose to place my trust and hope in You again today. I choose to live by faith not by sight. I choose to keep my eyes fixed on You and not on the waves. Help and strengthen me by Your Spirit to rise above the waves, for I will yet praise You, my God and my King.

Amen

Further reading

Psalm 42.

Chapter 9

GOD WILL PROVIDE

J ulia and I have experienced several seasons of scarcity and lack. Bringing up our large family of five children, losing my income, then going to Bible college and subsequently planting a church meant we had a period of approximately eight years when we had very little to live on. It was a really tough season. Even though we knew we were in the will of God it was pretty challenging at times.

There were many occasions when there was no money in the bank and payments were being declined. There was no food in the house, no petrol in the car and we still had all our bills to pay. We were so desperate on one occasion that we literally went for a walk and prayed that we would find some money on the pavement. We found nothing, but God provided in other ways. On another occasion we had no milk to feed our baby, so we had to ask someone to lend us a pound to buy it.

Our seasons of lack were often combined with pressures at church and work, poorly children, spiritual attacks, stress, anxiety and the normal challenges of bringing up five kids. Like most parents we wanted to give them the very best we could, but we dreaded them needing new shoes or school uniforms.

One thing we discovered was that having no money is pretty miserable. Unless you've been there you can't imagine the constant worry, anxiety and fear it creates. Having no money to buy presents for your kids at Christmas is just unbearable. We faced that scenario one year, but at the very last minute God suddenly and miraculously provided, as He so often does, and we were able to give them a great Christmas. God is good.

Can I just interrupt your reading to ask: is there anyone in your friendship circle, at work or at church who is struggling financially right now? If so, why don't you bless them? Do something really wonderful, and do it today! Be generous. Make their day. Imagine the difference you could make. Be the answer to their prayers...

I also really want to encourage those who are struggling right now. Perhaps you recently lost your job or business, or maybe you've seen your income decrease and life has become massively challenging as a result. Maybe there simply isn't enough money to cover the basic necessities. Perhaps you've run out of ways to rob Peter to pay Paul. Maybe you've had conversations with the bank and the creditors. I've been there, done that and experienced the humiliation. My heart goes out to you. So what can I encourage you to do?

First, tempting as it may be, please don't get into more debt. Cut up the credit cards and try to pay off as much of it as you can. Cut out all unnecessary spending and look for inexpensive ways to have fun and enjoy life. Your children will understand. Don't get into debt to keep them happy. Trust God that He will provide ways and means.

Second, guard your relationships by being transparent. No spouse wants to discover the full picture of poverty and mounting debt once it's already happened. Avoid unpleasant surprises by communicating well. Work on it together. Agree a tight budget. Having no money creates tension in the home, so make sure you guard those critical relationships. Love and encourage one another through this season, and don't blame each other for the position you have found yourself in. You will come through this.

Third, trust God deeply. You will learn to trust Him like never before in this season. In actual fact, you'll be better off in the future as your faith and trust will have increased so much. That was our experience, anyhow. So stay close to Him. Talk to Him. Pour out your heart to Him. Share your frustrations with Him. And pray together.

Remember this:

> "I was young and now I am old, yet I have never seen the righteous forsaken or their children begging bread" (Psalm 37:25).

Fourth, be thankful for small blessings. The big answers to prayer may not appear to be happening, and it's easy to become disenchanted with God. However, He is still at work behind the scenes; it may just take time for this season to pass. Sadly, Christians are not immune to the economic state of our countries or challenging job markets. God will come through, but find things you can be thankful for every day in the meantime. Learn to be content with what you have.

Fifth, pray like you have never prayed before. Commit to praying about your situation every day. Stand on His promises. List everything you need before God, and don't be afraid to ask for things that aren't necessarily essentials, such as holidays, trips, entertainment and toys. God is like any good Father; He loves to bless His children. A good father doesn't simply meet the most basic needs of his children.

We used to sit and pray as a family during our evening meal. We would thank God for everything we had and all that He was doing, then each child would bring a request to God. I believe this taught our kids a lot about faith, and they saw many prayers answered.

Sixth, wake up every morning expecting a miracle, and don't resort to eating your own children (see below!). They won't be very tasty and it could land you in serious trouble!

I love the story in 2 Kings 6 when Samaria was under siege from the armies of Ben-Hadad, King of Aram. The famine was so bad that the people started eating their own children. They were that desperate!

Within twenty-four hours God had turned the situation around. The next day, four lepers entered the camp of the Arameans. The Lord had caused the Arameans to hear the sound of chariots, horses and a great army, and they had fled for their lives, abandoning the camp along with all their food and belongings (see 2 Kings 7:5-16).

God unexpectedly broke through and ended the famine in a way no one expected, then the lepers, and subsequently the Israelites, plundered the camp. They must have enjoyed a wonderful feast. Can I encourage you to wake up each morning expecting God to provide?

He may not provide in the way you expect. I remember somebody arriving once, completely out of the blue, with a massive box of fruit and vegetables while Julia and I were at college. Another time, a church group brought round a carload of food. One year on our wedding anniversary £30 turned up unexpectedly and I was able to take Julia out for a meal. God will provide.

As I reflect back over the last thirty years, we have always been generous to God in giving to His Kingdom, and I have seen Him provide holidays, plane tickets to the US, food, clothing, nursery fees, school places, meals out, payments for trips and camps, cars, homes, debt clearance, college fees, mortgage payments, repair bills, jobs, church buildings, a minibus, equipment, Christmas presents and weddings. The list is endless.

He truly has proven Himself (as if He needed to) to be *Jehovah Jireh*, "the Lord will provide". I can confidently say, along with the apostle Paul, that:

"And this same God who takes care of me will supply all your needs from his glorious riches, which have been given to us in Christ Jesus" (Philippians 4:19, NLT).

He is faithful to keep His promises and loving towards all He has made. So don't be discouraged. Maintain your confidence, for God is your provider. Stand on this truth from scripture.

"I remain confident of this: I will see the goodness of the Lord in the land of the living. Wait for the Lord; be strong and take heart and wait for the Lord" (Psalm 27:13-14).

Father,

Forgive me for doubting You during this difficult season. Thank You that You are Jehovah Jireh, my provider. You are the God who will meet all my needs. Help me to trust You deeply at this time. Fill my heart with hope in the midst of lack, and peace when I feel anxious. Help me to see Your hand at work in the small details as well as in the big answers to prayer. Thank You that You never slumber nor sleep, and that You're working in the background for my good. Help me to remain expectant each day that You will provide.

Father, as I journey through this season, may I learn a great deal, but also help me not to forget those who are less fortunate than me. Help me to bless others even with the little that I have. May I put my faith into action for Your glory alone.

Amen

Further reading

Ephesians 3:20-21.

Chapter 10

CHOOSE JOY!

Don't you hate it when you lose something? We are forever losing things: keys, wallets, umbrellas, money and, most importantly of all, the TV remote! In fact, Julia is always complaining about losing the TV remote and asks me how it so often magically appears on the arm of the chair I'm sitting in.

We can so easily lose our joy, too. There are opportunities every day to become upset, frustrated and angry. People are rude; the traffic is horrendous, making us late; the Wi-Fi goes down at just the wrong moment, the coffee machine breaks, dinner is ruined; and the TV news... well, let's not even go there!

These are normal, everyday challenges, but for some reading this there may be bigger trials and challenges occurring. Some of these have dominated our thoughts for a long while and could continue to bring discouragement and frustration for a considerable amount of time to come. Nevertheless, we simply must not lose our joy.

My grandson was born a few weeks ago, in the middle of the lockdown period, and every time we see him on FaceTime he chuckles and grins at us. He is a happy and content little boy. He reminds me that, in the midst of all the challenges we are facing, God's desire is for us to enjoy a childlike faith, and that even as we go through some of the toughest trials we must choose joy.

Guarding your attitude

Chuck Swindoll writes: "You certainly cannot change the inevitable… What you can do is play on the one string that remains – your attitude. I am convinced that life is 10 percent what happens to me and 90 percent how I react to it. The same is true for you."[12]

We can't control the ten per cent. Stuff happens, traffic is bad and umbrellas go missing! However, we can control the other ninety per cent: our reaction to negative circumstances.

Didn't Nehemiah declare that "the joy of the Lord is your strength" (see Nehemiah 8:10)? If that's the case, it's clearly something we need to guard, protect and walk in every day. Joy is the second-listed fruit of the Spirit (Galatians 5:22-23), so it must be important. It needs to be central in our lives. Can I encourage you today to protect your joy? Let's try to see these trials as an opportunity to experience even greater joy.

> "My fellow believers, when it seems as though you are facing nothing but difficulties see it as an invaluable opportunity to experience the greatest joy that you can!" (James 1:2, TPT).

So what do we mean by joy?

The Collins English Dictionary defines it as: "A deep feeling or condition of happiness or contentment… something causing such a feeling; a source of happiness."[13] Theopedia describes it more convincingly as: "A state of mind and an orientation of the heart. It is a settled state of contentment, confidence and hope."[14]

Kay Warren writes:

"Joy is the settled assurance that God is in control of all the details of my life, the quiet confidence that ultimately everything is going to be alright, and the determined choice to praise God in all things."[15]

Whatever you are facing today, remember that God is in control. While everything around you may appear to be going wrong or falling apart, God continues to be in charge, so trust him deeply. Don't try to work it out for yourself; let Him guide you. Be assured that none of what you're experiencing has taken Him by surprise, and that He will either provide a way out or sustain you through it. The knowledge of this should bring fresh assurance that He is in control and cause you to rejoice.

Rejoice!

"Rejoice in the Lord always. I will say it again: rejoice! Let your gentleness be evident to all. The Lord is near. Do not be anxious about anything, but in every situation, by prayer and petition, with thanksgiving, present your requests to God. And the peace of God, which transcends all understanding, will guard your hearts and your minds in Christ Jesus" (Philippians 4:4-7).

Learn to focus on God and understand who He is. Worship Him during trials and difficulties, and choose (yes, it's a choice) to rejoice repeatedly. Say yes to being joyful in spite of everything you're going through. Be clear that this difficult season will not ruin your day or cause you to lose your joy. Declare that:

"This is the day the Lord has made. We will rejoice and be glad in it" (Psalm 118:24, NLT).

Hidden power

Joy is the hidden power of the Christian during a trial. It's more than a feeling; it is a deep confidence in God that allows us to worship, celebrate and be genuinely joyful no matter what our life circumstances seem to be telling us. Paul encourages the Roman believers to:

"Be joyful in hope, patient in affliction, faithful in prayer" (Romans 12:12).

Just recently I was privileged to conduct the funeral of a lovely man in our church who had died of terminal cancer, which he had battled for several years. His wife told me he had made a decision after the diagnosis to praise God no matter what, right until the very end. That is what they did, despite experiencing the darkest of seasons. It strengthened them and carried them through.

Henri Nouwen writes:

"People who have come to know the joy of God do not deny the darkness, but they choose not to live in it... Joy never denies the sadness, but transforms it to a fertile soil for more joy."[16]

Perhaps you are feeling anything but joyful today. That's OK, I've been there. Life can seem overwhelming at times, and tidal waves of negativity and sadness may flood our lives. But let me suggest three things you can do right now:

First, talk to him and:

"Give all your worries and cares to God, for He cares about you" (1 Peter 5:7, NLT).

David continually poured out his heart to God (see Psalm 62:8). I have done the same thing on numerous occasions, and it works.

Second, God has promised to fill you with joy:

> "You make known to me the path of life; you will fill me with joy in your presence, with eternal pleasures at your right hand" (Psalm 16:11).

Ask Him for it right now. Say: "Father God, please fill me with joy."

Third, never forget that God is at work. The One the Bible declares neither slumbers nor sleeps (see Psalm 121:1) is on your side and at work in your situation. He promises that:

> "Those who sow with tears will reap with songs of joy" (Psalm 126:5).

No matter what you're facing right now, and whatever today brings, refuse to lose your joy. Consider my smiling grandson and picture a baby full of joy. Breathe. Smile. Worship. Rejoice.

And remember this:

"The reward for choosing joy is joy itself."

Father,

I've been through so much lately and every day is a challenge. I feel like I've stopped trusting You with my life, and as a result I've lost my joy. I pray, as David did, that You would:

"Restore to me the joy of your salvation and grant me a willing spirit, to sustain me."[17]

Help me, in the midst of everything I'm facing to be the most joy-filled person I can be. I pray that people would see my life as an amazing testimony to Your grace and power. I declare that this is the day You have made, and that I will rejoice and be glad in it.

Amen

Further reading

Psalm 62.

Chapter 11

WHEN THE ENEMY COMES IN LIKE A FLOOD

During the winter of 2019, several towns in Yorkshire, England, were overwhelmed by torrential rain. The heavens opened and a month's worth of rain fell in just twenty-four hours, causing the water on the already sodden hills and in the overflowing streams to fill the towns in the valleys below with water. Streets, homes, businesses and shops were deluged, and any flood defences in place proved completely insufficient.

"O God, listen to my cry! Hear my prayer! From the ends of the earth, I cry to you for help when my heart is overwhelmed. Lead me to the towering rock of safety, for you are my safe refuge, a fortress where my enemies cannot reach me. Let me live forever in your sanctuary, safe beneath the shelter of your wings!" (Psalm 61:1-4, NLT).

Some theologians believe David wrote this psalm at the time of Absalom's rebellion. He was most likely feeling overwhelmed at the loss of his throne and the tabernacle, and, worse still, on discovering that his own son was leading the rebellion. He probably also wondered whether he would ever see his beloved Jerusalem again.

"When my anxious thoughts multiply within me,
Your consolations delight my soul" (Psalm 94:19, NASB).

I have always been pretty confident, optimistic and positive about life, genuinely hoping for the best. But I have to admit that I experienced a particular season in my ministry when I struggled for many months with an extremely challenging situation, a number of difficult people and a mind that was regularly filled with negative thoughts. These thoughts completely overwhelmed me at times, so I recognised how David must have felt as I read Psalm 61 one morning during my time with God. I think I could have written my own lament that day!

This psalm helped me recognise what was going on inside my head (people have probably been wondering about that for years!), and enabled me, through my journaling, to share these thoughts with my loving Father God. I wrote down thirteen reasons why I felt overwhelmed, covering my past, my present and my future. Identifying these areas really helped me and brought a great release. I felt set free. If you don't already journal, can I encourage you to start doing so?

Establishing flood defences

A barrier was built across the River Thames in 1974 to stop high tides causing severe flooding in central London. I believe there are seasons when we need to, with God's help, build flood defences around our lives in order to prevent us from becoming overwhelmed.

"…When the enemy comes in like a flood, The Spirit of the Lord will lift up a standard against him" (Isaiah 59:19, NKJV).

At times, the enemy of our souls will attack us from lots of different angles, using various people and situations. This can hit us like a flood, overwhelming our minds with negative thoughts, fears, anxiety and discouragement. He seeks to steal and kill; to destroy our faith and our lives (see John 10:10). He doesn't play fair and can be very convincing.

On these occasions we need to be alert to what is happening, but we can also ask the Spirit of God to lift up a standard against him and stop him in his tracks. When we do so the barrier goes up and the flooding stops. I have been there, and it works. I have cried out like David and seen God move.

"He reached down from on high and took hold of me; he drew me out of deep waters. He rescued me from my powerful enemy, from my foes, who were too strong for me. They confronted me in the day of my disaster, but the Lord was my support. He brought me out into a spacious place; he rescued me because he delighted in me" (Psalm 18:16-19).

It's OK to feel weak... you're in good company!

Another revelation I received as I read the words of David was that this great warrior king had moments when he felt overwhelmed, when he recognised that his enemies were too strong for him. It's almost inconceivable to think that one of the most outstanding warriors in scripture would admit that, and I found it really liberating. It's actually OK to feel weak and incapable of victory on occasion. God is OK with that.

In fact, Paul boasted about his weaknesses "so that Christ's power may rest on me... for when I am weak, then I am strong" (see 2 Corinthians 12:9-10). Isn't that amazing? Sometimes it's OK not to be a mighty man or woman of God. Sometimes it's OK to recognise our weakness.

In fact, it may be that it wasn't until David was willing to humble himself in that way that God mounted the incredible rescue mission dramatically described in this amazing psalm. We are fighting against a subtle and powerful enemy, but God is greater and stronger. Yes, we are on the victorious side, but sometimes we need to recognise and acknowledge that our enemy is simply too powerful for us. At such times we need to ask God to step in and rescue us, and He surely will.

There are occasions when the enemy will come in like a flood. Let's be quick to identify what is happening, humbling ourselves and allowing God to step in and rescue us. I penned the following prayer after talking to God about my life through my journal and listing all the things that had flooded my mind and overwhelmed me. You may want to use it as a basis for prayer before you do anything else today.

Father,

Reach down from on high and lift me out of the deep waters that threaten to overwhelm me. Rescue me from my powerful enemies, who are too strong for me.

I've been overwhelmed by my thoughts lately [list what has overwhelmed you]. Lord, can I please leave all these horrible, negative thoughts with You? I don't want to feel this way any more. I long to feel Your presence and anointing. I long to taste and see that You are good, and to enjoy my life and ministry again. Help me to keep the past in the past and allow You to do a new thing.

Father, please heal my damaged and hurting heart. Restore my heart of flesh. Wipe away my tears. Renew my mind. Grant me fresh courage and help me to obedient in all that You have called me to do. I declare that I have placed my hope in You, God, for I will yet praise You! I am convinced that this is true: better days lie ahead. All for Your glory, my precious heavenly Father.

Amen

Further reading

Psalm 18; Psalm 94:19; 1 Corinthians 4:9-13;
2 Corinthians 4:8-12; 16-18.

Chapter 12

FAITH, NOT FEAR

My wife Julia was a young widow when I first met her, and on our wedding day in September 1987 I 'inherited' three charming little boys. I not only became a husband but an instant dad! In fact I seem to remember that most of our early dates were spent in zoos, parks, adventure playgrounds and toy shops.

The early years of our marriage were a little difficult in that, having lost one husband, Julia was constantly fearful of losing the second one. So if I was late home from work or got talking to someone when I'd popped out for something from the local shop she would be filled with fear that something bad had happened to me. She told me that in her mind she would be convinced that I was dead and would already be planning my funeral, having shut all the curtains so no one could come to visit her. The issue of my being late (for whatever reason) actually caused a number of arguments because of the fear and stress Julia was experiencing.

Julia also felt she could never be truly happy, because she feared losing that happiness once again. In fact, when our daughter Sarah was born Julia was convinced she was going to die, to the point where she had regular dreams that Sarah was dying. Julia would wake up many times in the night to go and check on her. The fear was so real at times that she often felt physically sick.

I guess once something horrific occurs, such as losing your husband in an untimely death, you know that the very worst thing that could possibly happen does sometimes happen. It changes your perspective. Of course, our enemy the devil is always looking for opportunities to ensnare us in some way, and for Julia he used fear.

Thankfully, Julia was set free from her fear a long time ago. A friend prayed with her and encouraged her to "take captive every thought to make it obedient to Christ" (see 2 Corinthians 10:5). It hasn't been an issue since then, although I still occasionally get in trouble for being late!

You're not on your own; fear is common

You probably feel as though you're the only person who is suffering from fear, but as a pastor I've helped many people deal with their fears. There are some fairly common ones, such as fear of the dark, flying, heights, spiders, clowns, birds, needles, sickness, old age and death, as well as some less common ones.

The world is a fear-filled place, and all the more so during the Covid-19 pandemic we're currently experiencing. Many people are fearful right now. People are scared of the virus itself, of sickness, of death, of unemployment and of loss of income. Some are experiencing genuine fear for friends or family members. However, the Word of God declares:

> "Surely the righteous will never be shaken; they will be remembered for ever. They will have no fear of bad news; their hearts are steadfast, trusting in the Lord" (Psalm 112:6-7).

Where does fear come from?

> "For God will never give you the spirit of fear, but the Holy
> Spirit who gives you mighty power, love, and self-control"
> (2 Timothy 1:7, TPT).

The Bible is quite clear that it certainly doesn't come from God, but
rather the other fella! Fear is falsehood. It comes from the devil, who
is the enemy of our souls, the father of lies, and the destroyer of our
peace (see John 8:44). He masquerades as an angel of light. He loves
to spread fear, using lies to deceive God's people and causing them to
be fearful. He is an incredibly convincing deceiver at times, as I have
discovered on occasion.

I wonder what the enemy has convinced you of. What lies has he
planted in your head? What yarn has he spun for you? What lies do
you believe about yourself? What is your greatest fear?

Fear will rob you of your courage (making you *dis*couraged) and
of your life, purpose, hope, joy, peace, contentment, confidence
and boldness to obey God. Fear paralyses us, causing anxiety, stress,
sleepless nights, physical symptoms and other health issues.

Fear disables us, stopping us from becoming all that God has called
us to be. It stops us taking risks, stepping out in faith, fulfilling God's
plans and purposes for our lives, witnessing, serving and giving. Fear
controls and destroys lives. If left unchecked, fear will dominate our
minds and change our behaviour, impacting those closest to us.

But be encouraged today! God's desire is for us to live a fear-free
existence. His Word states:

> "So do not fear, for I am with you; do not be dismayed, for I
> am your God. I will strengthen you and help you; I will uphold
> you with my righteous right hand" (Isaiah 41:10).

God doesn't want us to be fear-filled people. He wants us to be *faith*-filled people! I want to encourage you to fight back today, and to determine not to allow fear to wreck your life or destroy your peace.

How do we fight back?

Here are some suggestions:

First, recognise his schemes. It is my firm conviction that the enemy knows me pretty well. He has identified my weaknesses and knows where I'm susceptible to attack. I believe he has a tailor-made scheme for me. Paul warned the Corinthians about the trap of unforgiveness, explaining it was a scheme the devil was using in their particular context (see 2 Corinthians 2:10-11).

Fear is another common strategy the enemy uses. It can develop from a simple circumstance in our lives, such as the examples below, or the enemy may plant a thought and then we begin to speculate. Before long we are caught in a cycle of anxiety and fear that started with a common situation or a seemingly unimportant thought.

For instance:

- That lump or pain in your body you've just noticed.

- That comment your boss made, which has been playing on your mind.

- That look from someone, which suggested they're not happy or that you may have a problem.

- That thought that has robbed you of the courage to step out and do all that God has placed in your heart to do.

Before long, you and I begin speculating about these things.

"Speculations prey upon our fears, seeking open doors in our lives through which they can lead us into bondage"[18] (Kris Vallotton).

We must not allow these speculations to hold us in bondage to fear. This is where a foothold (thought) can become a stronghold (control of the enemy) in our lives (see Ephesians 4:27).

Can you identify the schemes he is using in your life? What does he regularly use to trip you up and bring you down? What is your greatest recurring fear? The devil left Jesus alone until an opportune time. He usually waits until we're tired, hungry and weak. He often attacks when we're on the verge of a breakthrough or the fulfilment of a dream in a bid to make us give up.

Second, fight back. Joyce Meyer suggests that our minds are like battlefields. They are the places where the major battles are fought, and if we can win the battles in our minds we will live in victory! We must learn to take our thoughts captive and make them obedient to Christ, as Julia did.

Let's stop allowing the enemy to sow thoughts, doubts, fears and speculations into our hearts and minds! Let's take all thoughts that don't comply with God's Word of truth captive. Let's resist the devil until he flees from us (see James 4:7), remembering this:

"For God has not given us a spirit of fear, but of power and of love and of a sound mind" (2 Timothy 1:7, NKJV).

Let's win the battle of the mind, never forgetting that God has given us a sound mind (or self-control/self-discipline as some passages translate this verse). God has given you the tools to win this battle!

How do we do that? We pray, we submit our fear-filled thoughts to God and leave them with Him, and we stand on the truth of Scripture. Next, pray and ask God to give you a scriptural truth that counteracts the lie the enemy is trying to sow into your life. Declare it every day, and as often as you need to, in order to deny the fear the enemy is seeking to sow into your life. Do not allow it to take root.

No one else can do this for you. I have suffered with various fears during my lifetime. One in particular is recalled in my first book, *Imagine*, when for a period of approximately eight months I suffered from horrendous fears concerning my mental and physical health. These anxieties seriously debilitated me, having a massive impact on my life and ministry. I eventually got to a point where I chose to make a fight of it, helped by this quote:

"Courage is resistance to fear, mastery of fear – not absence of fear"[19] (Mark Twain).

Part of my deliverance came through my decision to say: "Fear, from now on I am your master. You won't be robbing me for a second longer. I'm choosing *faith*, not *fear*!"

Third, keep your perspective right. Let your perspective become a God perspective. It helps to focus on the good things Paul talks about in Philippians:

> "Finally, brothers and sisters, whatever is true, whatever is noble, whatever is right, whatever is pure, whatever is lovely, whatever is admirable – if anything is excellent or praiseworthy – think about such things" (Philippians 4:8).

We need to know the Bible and stand upon its truth when we feel fearful. Instead of thinking the worst, let's choose to believe God's Word. It's packed with promises and truth, which we can use to fight fear.

And don't forget to worship God. Worship brings us into God's presence. Worship causes the enemy to flee. Worship elevates us above everything that is threatening to bring us down. Worship releases faith, hope, joy, peace, strength, power, renewed courage and victory.

Let's be those who choose faith, not fear!

"Fear activates Satan's work in your life. In that same way, faith activates God's work in your life. Simply put, faith attracts God as fear attracts Satan. Fear becomes a conduit for Satan's destruction in your life. Faith is the conduit through which God's supernatural power flows into your life"[20] (Jentezen Franklin).

Choose faith, not fear.

Father,

The enemy came to steal, kill and destroy, but Jesus came that I might have life in all its abundance.[21] Please forgive me for walking in fear rather than in faith, and for believing lies rather than Your truth. I refuse to live in fear any longer. I reject every lie, speculation and fear the enemy has sown into my life [name specific ones].

I declare that You have not given me a spirit of fear, but of power, love and a sound mind.[22]

Today I choose faith over fear and truth over lies. I declare that I am now the master of my fears.

In Jesus' name,
Amen

NB: I pray these words or something similar over my life every day. I refuse to allow fear to master me any longer. I no longer live in fear, and all of my physical symptoms disappeared a long time ago.

Further reading

2 Corinthians 10:3-5; Philippians 4:4-9.

Chapter 13

BE FRUITFUL WHILE YOU WAIT

Horatio Spafford is perhaps an unfamiliar name to you. Various sources record that he was a successful lawyer and property investor in Chicago. He and his wife Anna had one son and four daughters, and they lived a life of philanthropy and service in their church until 1871. They lost their four-year-old son to scarlet fever that year, and a few months later the Great Chicago Fire wiped out the majority of their property holdings. Two years later Horatio lost his four daughters in an Atlantic shipwreck.

Later, as he was crossing the Atlantic to join his wife, he was inspired, as his ship neared the place where his daughters were lost, to write the words of one of the best-loved hymns of all time: "It Is Well With My Soul". He remained fruitful during a season of acute loss and suffering.

God's Word declares this:

> "'But blessed is the one who trusts in the Lord, whose confidence is in him. They will be like a tree planted by the water that sends out its roots by the stream. It does not fear when heat comes; its leaves are always green. It has no worries in a year of drought and never fails to bear fruit'" (Jeremiah 17:7-8).

Joseph's dreams

Joseph received two dreams from God. In the first he was binding sheaves of grain out in a field when all of a sudden his sheaf stood upright, while his brothers' sheaves gathered around his and bowed down to it. In the second dream the sun, moon and eleven stars bowed down to him (see Genesis 37:5-9).

As we know from the narrative, Joseph's lack of wisdom in sharing his dreams with his brothers caused them to become angry enough to sell him into slavery. Joseph initially served as a slave in Potiphar's house, and the Bible records that:

> "The Lord was with Joseph so that he prospered, and he lived in the house of his Egyptian master. When his master saw that the Lord was with him and that the Lord gave him success in everything he did, Joseph found favour in his eyes and became his attendant. Potiphar put him in charge of his household, and he entrusted to his care everything he owned. From the time he put him in charge of his household and of all that he owned, the Lord blessed the household of the Egyptian because of Joseph. The blessing of the Lord was on everything Potiphar had, both in the house and in the field. So Potiphar left everything he had in Joseph's care; with Joseph in charge, he did not concern himself with anything except the food he ate…" (Genesis 39:2-6).

Then, falsely accused of rape, Joseph was thrown into prison. While in prison, the Bible records that:

> "The Lord was with him; he showed him kindness and granted him favour in the eyes of the prison warder. So the warder put Joseph in charge of all those held in the prison, and he was made responsible for all that was done there. The warder paid no attention to anything under Joseph's care, because the Lord

was with Joseph and gave him success in whatever he did" (Genesis 39:21-23).

Joseph chose fruitfulness

The amazing part is that, while I suspect most of us would have sulked and felt sorry for ourselves, Joseph got his head down, worked hard and flourished. He was fruitful at a time in his life when he could have allowed despair and discouragement to control him.

In his later years, Jacob described his son Joseph as follows:

"'Joseph is a fruitful vine, a fruitful vine near a spring, whose branches climb over a wall. With bitterness archers attacked him; they shot at him with hostility. But his bow remained steady, his strong arms stayed supple, because of the hand of the Mighty One of Jacob, because of the Shepherd, the Rock of Israel, because of your father's God, who helps you, because of the Almighty, who blesses you with blessings of the skies above, blessings of the deep springs below, blessings of the breast and womb" (Genesis 49:22-25).

I don't believe God simply felt sorry for Joseph and decided to shower his life with favour because of the bad hand he had been dealt. No. It all started in Joseph's heart. This man, born to lead and full of vision, experienced control and confinement on two occasions, yet he kept his heart right and determined that he would serve others and be fruitful.

I have mentioned elsewhere that discouragement has the ability to rob us of courage and disable us in our lives and ministry. It is an odious thing and a tool the enemy uses to defeat us. However, we have a choice. We can choose to allow discouragement to negatively impact our lives or we can choose fruitfulness instead.

Choose fruitfulness

Daniel was fruitful during a time of exile in Babylon, and he exerted his godly influence. Nehemiah rebuilt the walls of Jerusalem while facing all kinds of opposition and attack. Esther influenced King Xerxes at a time of great persecution and oppression for her fellow Jews. Paul wrote some of his greatest epistles from a prison cell while awaiting almost certain death. John penned Revelation while in exile on the island of Patmos.

It seems to me that Jesus expects us to bear fruit no matter which season of our lives we find ourselves in. He said:

> "You did not choose me, but I chose you and appointed you so that you might go and bear fruit – fruit that will last..." (John 15:16).

How to be fruitful in your land of suffering

The way to be fruitful is to stay close to Him, the true vine, and allow Him to bear fruit in and through you. In fact, everlasting fruit is the Master's desire for our lives. In my experience, I have been unable to do anything of significance without or apart from Him.

Let's return to Joseph at the point when he was governor of Egypt:

> "Joseph named his firstborn Manasseh and said, 'It is because God has made me forget all my trouble and all my father's household.' The second son he named Ephraim and said, 'It is because God has made me fruitful in the land of my suffering.'" (Genesis 41:51-52).

The word 'trouble' can be defined as "misery", "affliction" and "poverty", according to *Strong's Concordance*[23]. It's a word with highly negative connotations, and it describes Joseph's early life very accurately.

However, Joseph clearly made the decision to forgive his brothers and Potiphar's wife, asking God to help Him forget the pain, suffering and rejection he had experienced. He determined that the past would not dictate the future, and that he would be fruitful in the land of his suffering.

Don't let your past, the suffering you're going through now or the challenges you're about to face diminish your fruitfulness for God. I wonder how or where can you become fruitful during this current season. What can you turn your hand to while you wait for things to change? Where is there a need that you can meet or a hurt that you can help heal? How could you use the passion, gifts, abilities and experiences God has placed within you to bless others? Where can you be fruitful in your land of suffering?

And who knows? Being fruitful through this difficult, discouraging season may well open the door to what God has planned for you next.

Father,

You know and understand everything I've been through, and everything I'm going through right now. It's been a really tough season. I forgive all those who have caused me heartache, pain and suffering. Enable me to let go of the past, to be courageous and to switch my focus to what I can do next. Give me fresh eyes to see Your vision for my life right now. Like Joseph and so many others, I choose to be fruitful in the land of my suffering, for Your praise and glory.

Amen

Further reading

John 15:1-17; Matthew 7:17-18; Galatians 5:22-25; Psalm 92:14.

Chapter 14

DON'T QUIT!

O ne of the greatest temptations in our lives is to quit. I suspect most of us have fought the desire to give up at some point. Perhaps you are in a season of discouragement and are asking yourself: "Why is this happening to me?" Maybe you are worn down from the battle you have just gone through or the difficult people you have faced or the apparent lack of success in what you've been doing. You may be wondering when, if ever, things will change.

Of course, there are some circumstances where quitting is absolutely appropriate and necessary, for example when it is quite clear that it is impossible for you to continue or for strategic reasons. A young athlete may realise that the 100-metre sprint needs to be put to one side because he or she is better at hurdles, for instance. In these cases, prayer and wise counsel is needed before any decision is made. However we must take care not to allow the general discouragements and difficulties of life to cause us to quit.

Warren W. Wiersbe writes:

"Others give up and turn back. But the child of God does not have to stop or go back; he can use the rocky places in life as stepping-stones to climb higher."[24]

> The apostle Paul must have been tempted to quit on many occasions. He must have fought discouragement, despondency and despair on an almost daily basis. If you have time, please give the many trials and challenges Paul experienced a read (see 2 Corinthians 1:8-11; 6:4-10; 11:23-29).

What a sobering list! He experienced hardships, beatings, imprisonment, danger, stonings, shipwreck, threats, hunger, thirst, cold, nakedness, sleeplessness, great pressure and even betrayal. Paul's life was constantly in danger, and he paid a huge price in order to share his faith.

You're in good company

I don't know what you're going through or what keeps you awake at night. Perhaps you recently received bad news. Maybe someone close to you has died, you've lost your job or you're experiencing financial difficulties. Perhaps you're battling ill health, an eating disorder, an unhappy marriage, a family crisis, anxiety or fear... or worse still, several of these at the same time.

Maybe like Paul you have moments when you despair of life itself and have reached a point where you can hardly bear to face tomorrow. It's been one thing after another, and you just don't know which way to turn. You may even be asking yourself: "What's the point?"

If so, you're in good company. If the great apostle could become so despondent and discouraged that he despaired of life itself, there is hope for us all! With God's help, Paul managed to keep going and work through it, and so can we.

Our great deliverer

I really want to encourage you with the truth that God promises to deliver us from or help us overcome the challenges we are facing. Paul said:

> "He has delivered us from such a deadly peril, and he will deliver us again. On him we have set our hope that he will continue to deliver us" (2 Corinthians 1:10).

Notice Paul's says: "He has *delivered* us" (past tense), "he *will deliver* us" (future tense) and "he *will continue to deliver* us" (future continuous tense). That's a lot of deliverance, but it just shows how important your life is to God. His commitment is to deliver us, past, present and future! So stand firm and wait for your deliverer. It will be worth the wait.

Set your hope on Him today. Don't quit. Don't give up on God. He hasn't changed. It is often the case that the longer a situation or period of suffering continues the more hopeless the situation can appear and the more discouraged we can become. You may be convinced that your struggle is going to last forever, but that's not true. He has sustained you this far and He will deliver you. He has promised to do so. Seasons change, storms pass, attitudes shift and resolutions are discovered. God can work in every situation and in every heart.

There is always hope

I've seen God's deliverance at various points in my life; practically, spiritually, emotionally and mentally. In 2007 I experienced a horrendous attack of mouth ulcers. This was something I had regularly suffered with since childhood, and no cure had been found. I had tried everything but nothing worked, nobody was able to help and it was really impacting my life. It's very difficult being a pastor and a preacher when you can't speak because you're in excruciating pain.

On this particular occasion the situation was so bad that my whole mouth had become one massive ulcer. I couldn't talk, eat, drink or sleep, and I was losing weight. Julia found me crying in our bathroom during the middle of the night because I was in such agony. Each day I kept hoping it would end, but it actually became much worse, to the point where I was admitted to Aintree Hospital in Liverpool. The consultant was so shocked at the state of my mouth that he asked if he could take photos to show his medical students!

I never lost hope that my mouth would get better. Although it was a painful and debilitating experience, I absolutely trusted that God would eventually deliver me. I had spoken to every doctor and expert I could find over the years, but during my hospital stay I was referred to a specialist who almost immediately recognised what was causing the problem. Within a few days I was 100 per cent better, and I have never suffered with mouth ulcers since. Thank you, Jesus! He is our deliverer. Can I encourage you to set your hope on Him and no one else today?

Sometimes we can get to the end of ourselves when we pray. When this happens, we simply need to ask for help and invite others to pray us through the situation we have found ourselves in. Paul reminds us of the importance of praying for one another:

> "And pray in the Spirit on all occasions with all kinds of prayers and request. With this in mind, be alert and keep on praying for all the Lord's people" (Ephesians 6:18).

Air support

My son used to play *Call of Duty* on his Xbox. I was watching him play one day, and he said: "Look, Dad, I can call in air support!"

He demonstrated how the ground troops occasionally needed backup to win the battle. Within moments of being called upon, fighter jets arrived and blitzed the enemy. Perhaps it's time you called in some extra spiritual fire power.

Wesley Duewel writes: "Prayer is the final armament! Prayer is the all-inclusive strategy of war. It is a form of spiritual bombing to saturate any area before God's army of witnesses begin their advance. Prayer is the all-conquering, invincible weapon of the army of God."[25]

I've come to realise that there are occasions when I need to be willing to humble myself and say these words to someone: "Please will you pray for me?" In fact, the following words would be even more appropriate: "Please will you pray for me every day until this situation changes? Will you pray me through it?"

Don't forget who is praying for you!

If you're feeling discouraged and ready to quit today, consider one final thing. Jesus is praying for you and interceding before the Father on your behalf (see Romans 8:34 and Hebrews 7:25). He said this to Simon Peter:

> "'Simon, Simon, Satan has asked to sift all of you as wheat. But I have prayed for you, Simon, that your faith may not fail. And when you have turned back, strengthen your brothers'" (Luke 22:31-32).

Jesus prayed Simon Peter through his time of testing and suffering. How awesome is that? Whatever you're going through, Jesus is praying for you right now. As you face a host of problems or challenges, as you lie in hospital, experience the loss of a career, face bereavement, tackle a mountain of debt, receive a life-changing diagnosis or begin to face life on your own and don't know which way to turn, remember that Jesus is praying for you.

Jesus warned us that we will all go through tough times: "...'In this world you will have trouble. But take heart! I have overcome the world'" (John 16:33).

I feel so encouraged when I read these words from Luke and John. Sadly, some people go through things that shake the very foundations of their faith. If you feel this way, never forget that Jesus is praying you through.

So let me encourage you not to quit today, no matter how bad things look. Keep going!

Father,

I've been so discouraged and overwhelmed by everything I've been facing lately. These issues seem to have been going on forever. Thank You that I'm in good company with the saints of old, who kept going and refused to quit. Help me not to quit while I wait for Your deliverance. In fact, help me to flourish!

Thank You that there is a fresh reservoir of strength and courage available every day. Please come and fill me with Your power and that inner strength that says: "With God's help, I will keep going and not quit!"

In Jesus' name,
Amen

Further reading

Psalms 13, 18, 40 and 140.

Chapter 15

HE RESTORES OUR SOULS

I went through a particular season of great discouragement as a pastor. The church I was leading wasn't growing and I didn't seem to be making any headway with our building project. I guess I had put a lot of pressure on myself to complete what I'd started, but I just wasn't able to get things moving or create any momentum. My solution was to work harder and harder, resulting in fatigue and despair. So what did I do at that point? I worked even harder.

It wasn't until one of my close friends said to me: "Simon, you need to take a day off!" that I realised my personal weariness wasn't helping me or the church. As soon as I started to rest properly and take some time out the discouragement began to lift and my energy levels started to rise. I began to see things from a fresh perspective and felt energised to keep the project moving in the right direction.

Right from the beginning to the very end of the Bible, God has encouraged His people to rest. To enjoy a sabbath rest. To not become weary or heavily burdened with life. It's so easy to just keep working, but one thing the pandemic has forced many of us to do is get off the hamster wheel and take life a bit more slowly. Rest needs to be built into the rhythm of our lives if we're to avoid becoming weary, burned out and discouraged. It's OK to rest.

Psalm 23 focuses on rest:

> "The Lord is my Shepherd [to feed, to guide, and to shield me], I shall not want. He makes me lie down in green pastures; He leads me beside the still *and* quiet waters. He refreshes *and* restores my soul (life)..." (Psalm 23:1-3, AMP).

I love a good restaurant

Nothing beats a good meal out for me. Interestingly, the verb we have translated as 'restore' from Psalm 23 comes from French word 'restaurant'. Were you aware that every time you go out for a meal something spiritual is happening? Restoration is happening. That's so good, and it makes me feel much better about the occasional overindulgence!

We all need to allow time for our souls to be restored. It's clear that we're more than mere lumps of moulded dust. There is an inner essence; a soul that has been made in the very image of God himself. It is the central part of who we are, and it is from this that our very life flows.

Rest and restoration

God's desire is to restore our souls; to restore our very lives. I believe there are two aspects to this: rest and restoration.

We all need time to rest. To take it easy. To stop working and doing. To have a nap. To take a break. To do nothing at all. Some of us find this easier than others!

Reflecting on his life, David declares in Psalm 23 that God refreshes and restores his soul. The Message version translates his words as "you let me catch my breath" and "you revive my drooping head".

I love one of the stories in Lettie Cowman's *Springs in the Valley*:

"In the deep jungles of Africa, a traveler was making a long trek. [Natives] had been engaged from a tribe to carry the loads. The first day they marched rapidly and went far. The traveler had high hopes of a speedy journey. But the second morning these jungle tribesmen refused to move. For some strange reason they just sat and rested. On inquiry as to the reason for this strange behavior, the traveler was informed that they had gone too fast the first day, and that they were now waiting for their souls to catch up with their bodies."[26]

Sometimes we need to catch our breath and let our souls catch up with our bodies!

Jesus withdrew

In the midst of a heavy schedule of ministry, Jesus regularly withdrew from the crowds with all their demands in order to rest:

"Then, because so many people were coming and going that they did not even have a chance to eat, he said to them, 'Come with me by yourselves to a quiet place and get some rest.' So they went away by themselves in a boat to a solitary place" (Mark 6:31-32).

"But Jesus often withdrew to lonely places and prayed" (Luke 5:16).

You have Jesus' permission and encouragement to rest.

Sometimes we too will need to withdraw from the busyness of our constantly connected age. It can be done if we're disciplined and let everyone know we're having some time out and will be turning everything electrical off. We will feel more energised as a result. Perhaps it's time for you to catch your breath.

Recreation time

While it's important to pause and rest, I believe recreation is a God-given gift that aids our restoration. Doing the things we enjoy and are passionate about is so important. It might be playing sport or watching our favourite teams play, or it might be walking, dancing, gardening, reading, art or whatever hobby we most enjoy. Recreation involves doing the things that inspire us and make our hearts leap.

When was the last time you did something you really enjoyed? Why don't you plan that visit, learn that instrument, take up that sport, join that club, book those tickets, see that show, plan that trip or organise that holiday of a lifetime? Do something you've never done before. Have some fun. Recreate yourself!

Moving back to the point of departure

There is an even greater depth of meaning to the verb 'restore'. While some have suggested that the soul is refreshed by God, the word's roots indicate a "movement back to the point of departure".[27] Perhaps it's time to stop doing and going, and to return to where God wants us to be, either in a physical or spiritual sense. It is so easy, in the busyness of life, to lose our way and depart from who we truly are. Of course, there are many things that may contribute to this.

I'm sure David experienced frustration, lack, fear, anxiety and stress at times, as well as the never-ending demands of his people and his kingship. He was a warrior king and had many enemies. He faced sadness, regret, rejection, death, loss, guilt and shame. He sinned and was sinned against.

All these things have the potential to damage our souls and to affect our mental well-being. They take away from who we are. They change our hearts and personalities. We may not initially notice, but those around us will have. David eventually recognised he had lost something. I suspect that this great worshipper and king had lost his way spiritually. Life had drawn him away from his first love and his passion for God. I'm sure he was able to identify when this occurred (perhaps when he sinned with Bathsheba), and he clearly desired God to bring restoration:

"Restore to me the joy of my salvation and grant me a willing spirit, to sustain me" (Psalm 51:12).

Perhaps, like David, you feel as though you've lost your way. If so, maybe you need to identify your point of departure and ask God to restore whatever it is you've lost. It's almost as though there are moments when we need a factory reset. At times like this we should ask God to work in our hearts, bringing healing, restoration and renewal as only He can.

Returning to the passage in Psalm 23, this is what Jesus, the Good Shepherd, desires to minister into your life:

"The Lord is my best friend and my shepherd. I always have more than enough. He offers a resting place for me in his luxurious love. His tracks take me to an oasis of peace, *the quiet brook of bliss*. That's where he restores and revives my life…" (Psalms 23:1-3, TPT).

Could it be that one of the exit routes from discouragement right now is to allow God to restore your soul? I guess the main question is: what needs restoring, recreating or re-establishing in your life? Perhaps you feel as though something has died inside you or there's something missing. Perhaps you've lost your passion for a relationship, marriage, project, job or area of service you used to love, or you just feel as though you're not the person you used to be.

Maybe it's time to move back to the point of departure. Maybe you need to retrace your steps, asking God to show you what happened and where you have been knocked off course, and for a full system restoration. Maybe you need simply to rest and enjoy some recreation. Maybe you need a fresh touch from God. Remember that He is the One who restores our souls.

Father,

I've lost my way somehow. I've changed. I'm weary and worn out. I've lost my passion. Please lead me beside still waters to rest and be restored. Heal my heart, lift off any heaviness and renew me by transforming my mind. Restore to me the joy of my salvation and give me a willing spirit to sustain me. Enable a renewed me to emerge from this season.

In Jesus' name,

Amen

Further reading

Psalms 23 and 71.

Chapter 16

COURAGE TO BE YOURSELF

It was another ordinary day. Autumn leaves were beginning to cover the ground, the weather was cloudy and damp, and there were the usual pressures of getting five children off to school prior to heading to the college chapel for morning devotions. I have to admit I struggled during those early months at Bible college, surrounded by people who seemed far more spiritual and knowledgeable than me. In fact, I felt inferior, intimidated and out of place. I was also tempted to copy those around me at times in an attempt to fit in.

Little did I know that God was about to speak some words into my heart that would change my life forever, releasing me to serve his purposes. The speaker that day was our director of studies, Dr Siegfried Schatzmann. I'm not entirely sure what the subject was, but at some point in his message he read these life-changing words from Paul:

"For I am the least of the apostles and do not even deserve to be called an apostle, because I persecuted the church of God. But by the grace of God I am what I am, and his grace to me was not without effect. No, I worked harder than all

of them – yet not I, but the grace of God that was with me"
(1 Corinthians 15:9-10).

Life change

In that moment I realised, for the first time, that God loved me exactly as I was, and that he simply wanted me to be myself, or at least the best me I could be. Paul had been a really horrible person. He had persecuted the early Church, and he'd arranged for godly people to be thrown into prison and even killed. He was present when Stephen was martyred. God revealed to me that if, with His help, Paul could get over that and be everything God had called him to be, so could I.

I made a very clear decision that day. I decided I was not going to be intimidated by the great theologians and spiritual giants around me for a second longer (many of them are among my closest friends today) and that I was simply going to enjoy being myself. Paul said: "I am, what I am." He refused to compare himself with the other apostles or to compete with them.

I came to terms with that fact and determined to focus on my strengths rather than my weaknesses. Rather than comparing myself, copying others or conforming to what people expected me to be or do, I was simply going to be the person God had made me. I was going to be comfortable in my own skin. I was going to have the courage to be myself.

As E.E. Cummings suggests:

"To be nobody-but-yourself – in a world which is doing its best, night and day, to make you everybody else – means to fight the hardest battle which any human being can fight; and never stop fighting."[28]

I was determined to make the most of the life and breath God had given me.

Liberty, not licence

This fresh revelation didn't mean I could behave badly or selfishly. In fact, quite the contrary. As Paul says in 1 Corinthians 15:10:

"…And his grace to me was not without effect. No, I worked harder than all of them – yet not I, but the grace of God that was with me." It's important to note that Paul, feeling free in spite of his past, relied on God's grace and power to become the best Paul he could be.

This is what I wrote in my journal that day:

"I cannot be anyone else – it's no use watching others or trying to be what others are. I have decided to be MYSELF and, by God's grace, to be and become what He has called me to be" (9th October 1993).

I think I do a pretty good 'Simon Lawton' these days. He likes football, running, Marmite, American hard gums, mince pies, James Bond and *Die Hard*. He dislikes cooking, DIY, hoovering and gardening. In fact, I would go even further and say that I've become quite amazing at simply being Simon Lawton rather than trying to be someone else (although my wife may still not be particularly impressed by this!).

Joking aside, I'm a work in progress. My constant prayer is that God will change and transform me, and that I will become more Christlike. One of my recurring personal prayers is that the fruit of the Spirit will become more visible in my life:

"But the fruit of the Spirit is love, joy, peace, forbearance, kindness, goodness, faithfulness, gentleness and self-control…" (Galatians 5:22-23).

Be yourself!

Can I encourage you to be yourself? Be the person God went to all the trouble of so beautifully creating…

"For you created my inmost being; you knit me together in my mother's womb. I praise you because I am fearfully and wonderfully made; your works are wonderful, I know that full well. My frame was not hidden from you when I was made in the secret place, when I was woven together in the depths of the earth. Your eyes saw my unformed body; all the days ordained for me were written in your book before one of them came to be" (Psalm 139:13-16).

Don't compare

Don't compare yourself with others. I've been guilty of this at times in my ministry, and I believe most of us do it at some point. We can so easily become frustrated and dissatisfied with who we are and start wishing we were taller, slimmer, funnier, more intelligent, more gifted, more charismatic, more confident… the list goes on.

The simple truth is this: you cannot change what God has created, for example your appearance, height, intellect, upbringing, personality, past experiences, gifts or abilities. You can only build on and develop these attributes. Be encouraged today that God thought you were worth creating, and that He uniquely shaped you for His purposes. You have the rest of your life ahead of you, so learn to accept it and enjoy the journey of being you. No one else can do it the way you can!

If you try to be someone else we'll all miss out and you will fail to fulfil the purpose God created you for, which will only lead to frustration and disappointment. The world doesn't need another Simon Lawton; it simply needs you to be *you*!

"Be yourself; everyone else is already taken" (provenance unknown).

As I look back over the past twenty-plus years since that ordinary day when God brought about that life change, I am so grateful that He cared enough to speak into my life. We must each grasp that we are uniquely shaped by God to be used for His eternal purposes. He actually takes great pleasure in who we are and what, with His help, we will become.

This became a life-impacting message for me, and I hope it will give you the courage to free yourself from trying to be something you're not and to become all that God has destined for you instead.

Why don't you make my journal comment your prayer right now?

Father God,

I cannot be anyone else. It's no use watching others or trying to be what others are. I have decided today to be myself and, by Your grace, to be and become what You have called me to be.

Please help me, Father God.

Amen

Further reading

2 Peter 1:1-10; Colossians 3:1-17.

Chapter 17

CYNICISM

T he Cynics were a group of fourth-century BC Greek philosophers who rejected conventional living in preference of a simpler, more natural life. Some lived on the streets of Greece. They rejected power, possessions, money, fame and shelter, and were anti-state, anti-democracy and anti-capitalism. They were the early anarchists.

Cynicism has naturally declined over the centuries to become a disbelief in the sincerity of human actions. The Oxford English Dictionary describes a cynic as: "A person who believes that people are motivated purely by self-interest rather than acting for honourable or unselfish reasons."[29]

The Merriam-Webster defines the word 'cynical' as: "Contemptuously distrustful of human nature and motives."[30]

There is a suggestion that the older we get the more cynical we become. In fact, I've realised that cynicism can creep up on people just as easily as middle-age spread. It's easy to miss it until your jeans suddenly become a little too tight! However, cynicism can hit us at any stage of our lives, however, and it:

- Assumes the worst possible motives for people's behaviour.

- Suggests we have lost all hope of better days ahead.

- Implies that our past experiences will continue into our present and future.

- Expects that the light at the end of the tunnel is, in fact, a heavily loaded freight train heading in our direction!

- Says that things will never get better.

- Questions everything.

- Sees everything and everyone from a negative viewpoint.

- Responds with sarcasm and judgement.

- Doesn't believe in a happy ever after.

- Kills faith, expectation and belief in God and others.

- Has the potential, when shared with others, to bring them down.

Have you become cynical?

Perhaps you hadn't realised how cynical you have become. So how did you end up in this place? I think sometimes in our sanitised Western version of Christianity we have been (wrongly) led to believe that we will constantly live in great victory, health and wealth, and that every aspect of our lives will be perfect. Those of us who are a bit older know that this isn't the reality.

Perhaps your belief in the goodness of people, humanity or the world has become eroded over time because of the horrible things you have seen happening around you. Perhaps you've been on the receiving end of some of those horrible things. Maybe you've been hurt or had your heart broken once too often. When the reality of this world with all its messed-up people (including you and me!), imperfections and lack hits home it can lead to massive disappointment.

Cynicism can be a sign of unrealised hopes, unfulfilled promises or unanswered prayers. In Genesis, Sarah laughed – a form of cynicism – when the angel declared she would become pregnant at the ripe old age of ninety:

> "Then one of them said, 'I will return to you about this time next year, and your wife, Sarah, will have a son!' Sarah was listening to this conversation from the tent. Abraham and Sarah were both very old by this time, and Sarah was long past the age of having children. So she laughed silently to herself and said, 'How could a worn-out woman like me enjoy such pleasure, especially when my master – my husband – is also so old?'" (Genesis 18:10-12, NLT).

Cynicism may be a sign that you've been through a particularly difficult and challenging season. Or perhaps you have experienced a series of tough seasons; one after another after another. "Where is God?" you may have been tempted to ask.

Cynicism may be a sign that you no longer trust people or God. Perhaps you have been gravely sinned against, ill-treated, abused, misrepresented, let down, rejected or lied about. Maybe you've made an inner vow that you will never trust anyone again. We must guard our hearts from such vows, which ultimately hurt us more than other people anyway.

Battling cynicism

How can you battle cynicism on those days when discouragement, disillusionment and despair come knocking at your door? Perhaps these pointers will help:

- Guard your heart. It is the wellspring of life (see Proverbs 4:23).

- Reset your expectations of others. Are they higher than the ones you are imposing on yourself?

- Recognise that the world is a sin-filled and sin-tarnished place, and that we are all tainted by and have played our part in it.

- Recognise that people, companies and governments will let you down.

- Understand that not all Christians behave like Christians. In fact, pastors and leaders are also sinners. They may make mistakes and get things wrong, even if their intentions are good.

- Remember that you're not so great either! Stop being so self-righteous (I've often had to remind myself of this!).

- Choose to see the very best in everyone and to judge others (if you must!) by their intentions rather than by their actions.

- Show mercy, grace and compassion towards others.

- Don't keep a record of wrongs, but rather think the very best of everyone around you (see 1 Corinthians 13:4-7).

- Choose positivity and reject negativity.

- Let go of the past. Talk to God about it if you need to, then leave it with Him.

- Swap disappointment, disillusionment and discouragement for faith, hope and joy.

Paul has some great advice for us here:

"Therefore, as God's chosen people, holy and dearly loved, clothe yourselves with compassion, kindness, humility, gentleness and patience. Bear with each other and forgive one another if any of you has a grievance against someone. Forgive as the Lord forgave you. And over all these virtues put on love, which binds them all together in perfect unity" (Colossians 3:12-14).

There have been many times as a pastor when I have experienced the very worst of people as well as the very best. I have also seen what humans can do to their fellow humans. However, I have realised that we must simply make a choice to keep our hearts right. We are the guardians of our own souls – no one else can fulfil this role – and each of us is accountable to the Father.

Make a decision to let go of all that horrible cynicism today. It is draining and negative, and it will taint your view of this wonderful world. It will also taint your view of the amazing people around you, many of whom are on your side, care deeply about you, and are trying to help you succeed in life and become everything God has called you to be.

Father,

Please forgive me for allowing my heart to become so cynical. Just as a car engine needs a service and fresh oil, I ask You to cleanse my innermost being and fill me with fresh, pure oil. Take away all the dirt and debris from my heart. Remove all the bitterness, hardness, hurt, disappointment, disillusionment, frustration, anger, envy, sadness, rejection, judgement, sarcasm, doubt, fear, bad memories and lack of trust in people and their motives. In fact, remove anything that is hindering my walk with You and my relationships with others.

Please restore my faith in You and in people, and fill my heart with fresh joy. Help me to believe the best in everyone and everything.

Amen

Further reading

Ephesians 4:17-32; Psalm 51; Ezekiel 36:26-27.

Chapter 18

KEEP MOVING!

My daughter came to stay one Easter and challenged me to do my first parkrun (5K) with her in the picturesque Cannon Hill Park in Birmingham. I really enjoyed it, though technically it included several stops due to my lack of stamina... and I thought I was fit! My daughter returned to her own home after a few days, but I'd already caught the running bug. I now enjoy running so much that I've given up my gym membership and I run 5K a couple of times per week in addition to the weekly parkrun. Every now and then I even get a PB!

However, some mornings I really struggle to motivate myself and put my running gear on. It's a challenge to get myself moving and sometimes to keep myself moving. I can come up with all kinds of excuses – the weather, tiredness, busyness and a sore knee – that could potentially stop me heading out of the front door, and if I leave it for a few days it becomes even harder to get back out there.

Paul challenged the Philippians with these words:

"I'm not saying that I have this all together, that I have it made. But I am well on my way, reaching out for Christ, who has so wondrously reached out for me. Friends, don't get me wrong: By no means do I count myself an expert in all of this, but I've got my eye on the goal, where God is beckoning us onward – to Jesus. I'm off and running, and I'm not turning back.

"So let's keep focused on that goal, those of us who want everything God has for us. If any of you have something else in mind, something less than total commitment, God will clear your blurred vision – you'll see it yet! Now that we're on the right track, let's stay on it." (Philippians 3:12-16, MSG).

Discouragement can debilitate us, causing our momentum to stop. It has the potential to draw us into a hole from which we struggle to escape. It can cause us to withdraw, diminish our productivity and destroy our creativity. We mustn't allow it to! We must not allow the enemy of our souls to wreck our lives and reduce our potential in Christ.

When I feel discouraged I actively choose to do something to get myself moving again. I always pray. I remember all the good things in my life. I worship if I'm able to. But I've also discovered that I need to get moving again. I have to get those running shoes back on and rejoin the race. I have to choose each day that discouragement will not win, and it's a choice that only I can make.

According to The Franklin Institute, Thomas Edison developed at least three thousand theories before creating a workable lightbulb. Can you imagine how discouraging that must have been? Can you imagine all the negative comments? "Thomas, you're wasting your time" and "It'll never happen!". However, Edison didn't allow himself to become discouraged. According to the institute, he later wrote:

"The electric light has caused me the greatest amount of study and has required the most elaborate experiments… I was never myself discouraged, or inclined to be hopeless of success. I cannot say the same for all my associates."[31]

Edison refused to give in to discouragement, even when those around him desired to quit. He kept moving forward and eventually achieved his goal. I guess there have been many times when people have quit too early. However, I'm convinced that some of the most important things in the world have been accomplished by those who refused to stop trying even when the situation looked hopeless.

So don't quit! It's time to stop dwelling on what might have been or what hasn't yet happened and get moving again.

When children are learning to ride a bicycle they often fall off a few times before they master it. Most parents will encourage them to get back on their bikes as soon as possible, encouraging them not to be scared of falling off again and telling them that they can, and will, master cycling.

Perhaps it's time for you to get back on your bicycle. You may be a bit sore and bruised, and you may need to pick yourself up off the floor, dust yourself down and get going again, ignoring the discouraging words of others, the negative voices in your head and the circumstances you find yourself in. As you already know, nothing of true value in this world is gained without a bit of courage and hard work.

Neil A. Maxwell said: "Discouragement is not the absence of adequacy but the absence of courage." So why not ask God for some fresh courage to replace the discouragement today? And once you've done that, get moving!

What can you do to get back on your bike? What have you put down that you need to pick up again? What is the next step you need to take in order to achieve your dream? It may be time to take on a new challenge; to ask God for the courage you need and finally go for it; to do what you've always wanted to do.

How about making plans and taking a few small steps towards that dream? I didn't write this book in one weekend, you know. I'm a lead pastor with many responsibilities. I also have five children and six grandchildren. I'm a busy man. I made a plan, then wrote the book one day at a time over a period of about six months. And of course the editorial, cover design and marketing stages followed that. Whatever you're hoping to achieve might seem massive and scary right now, so what small action steps can you plan for and begin to take?

As John Maxwell said: "Courage can be in the small choices that we make each day, in doing something despite being afraid of it."[32]

So do something courageous today. Step out. Start moving towards your dream. You never know; it might be the key that unlocks the door to untold blessing for you and many others. It may even reveal the very reason you are alive.

I'm always encouraged by these words from Hebrews:

> "Do you see what this means – all these pioneers who blazed the way, all these veterans cheering us on? It means we'd better get on with it. Strip down, start running – and never quit! No extra spiritual fat, no parasitic sins. Keep your eyes on *Jesus*, who both began and finished this race we're in. Study how he did it. Because he never lost sight of where he was headed – that exhilarating finish in and with God – he could put up with anything along the way: Cross, shame, whatever. And now he's *there*, in the place of honor, right alongside God. When you find yourselves flagging in your faith, go over that story again, item by item, that long litany of hostility he plowed through. *That* will shoot adrenaline into your souls!" (Hebrews 12:1-3, MSG).

Discouragement causes us to lose our courage. It debilitates us, causing us to play safe and avoid taking risks. The antidote? Get moving again and keep moving!

Father,

I make a choice today to stop listening to the negative voices in my life. I will not allow myself to be incapacitated by the lies of the enemy, or to miss my opportunity to be all that You have created me to be. It's time to get moving again. This world needs me to be me and, with Your help, the best me that I can be.

I ask You for fresh energy and courage to run this race of life. Fill me, inspire me and help me to take the steps You're calling me to take today.

In Jesus' name
Amen

Further reading

Isaiah 40:28-31; Jeremiah 29:11.

Chapter 19

BE STRONG AND COURAGEOUS

Every time I read the early part of Joshua and Gideon's stories I'm struck by their humanness. Both biblical legends needed to receive encouraging words from God. In fact, Joshua, Gideon and Solomon (whom we will read about a little later) all needed to hear words like this:

> "'Be strong and courageous, because you will lead these people to inherit the land I swore to their ancestors to give them. Be strong and very courageous. Be careful to obey all the law my servant Moses gave you; do not turn from it to the right or to the left, that you may be successful wherever you go... Have I not commanded you? Be strong and courageous. Do not be afraid; do not be discouraged, for the Lord your God will be with you wherever you go'" (Joshua 1:6-9).

Joshua had heard the same words from Moses when he was commissioned as Moses' successor:

> "'Be strong and courageous. Do not be afraid or terrified because of them, for the Lord your God goes with you; he will never leave you nor forsake you.' Then Moses summoned

Joshua and said to him in the presence of all Israel, 'Be strong and courageous, for you must go with this people into the land that the Lord swore to their ancestors to give them, and you must divide it among them as their inheritance. The Lord himself goes before you and will be with you; he will never leave you nor forsake you. Do not be afraid; do not be discouraged'" (Deuteronomy 31:6-8).

Five times Joshua was exhorted to be strong and courageous before he commenced the conquest of the Promised Land.

I suspect we also need to demonstrate both of these attributes. Having courage without the strength to carry through what God has called you to do is not enough, and having strength with no courage will see little happen apart from the flexing of a few muscles. This is not dissimilar to a body-building competition. The contenders may look amazing, but very little is really achieved!

Unpacking Joshua's story

Joshua's story is encouraging for us all. It suggests to me that he was neither feeling strong nor full of courage. He had spent years as an intern serving Moses, watching one of Israel's greatest leaders at work from close at hand. He'd seen the Israelites at their worst. He had shared the challenges and frustrations of leadership and now it was his turn; not just to rule Israel, but to lead the people into many battles until the Promised Land was secured.

I'm sure we all feel like Joshua at times. He clearly felt weak and was lacking in courage. This was not a great combination for the new leader of Israel, who was about to take the people across the Jordan to fight huge enemies, according to the spies:

"...They said, 'The land we explored devours those living in it. All the people we saw there are of great size. We saw the

Nephilim there (the descendants of Anak come from the Nephilim). We seemed like grasshoppers in our own eyes, and we looked the same to them'" (Numbers 13:32-33).

What can we learn?

There are many things we can learn from this narrative. First, If you're attempting to doing anything of consequence, discouragement will come as surely as night follows day. Discouragement is a powerful weapon of Satan, who will do anything he can to intimidate us, make us fearful and cause us to lose our enthusiasm, confidence and courage to press into all that God has for us.

Don't allow anyone or anything to discourage you. Stay focused on the prize. Learn from Nehemiah who, while attempting to rebuild the walls of Jerusalem was constantly hearing negative comments and letters. He experienced opposition, scheming threats and intimidation. On one occasion his enemies tried to entrap him, but his response was:

"…'I'm doing a great work; I can't come down. Why should the work come to a standstill just so I can come down to see you?'" (Nehemiah 6:3, MSG).

That should also be our attitude. Let nothing stop you doing what God has called you to do.

Second, it's OK to feel weak, afraid and lacking in courage at times. God can still use you. In fact, I think He prefers to use those of us who recognise that we haven't got it all together. I'm not sure He's particularly into the super saints with everything completely worked out. Gideon is a prime example of someone who wasn't quite there:

"The Lord turned to him and said, 'Go in the strength you have and save Israel out of Midian's hand. Am I not sending you?' 'Pardon me, my lord,' Gideon replied, 'but how can I save Israel? My clan is the weakest in Manasseh, and I am the least in my family'" (Judges 6:14-15).

All God desired was for Gideon to go in the strength he had. And that's all He requires of you today; to go in whatever strength you have. He will provide everything else you need. My knowledge and experience of God is that where He calls, He also equips. It also reminds me that He is more than able to fight my battles, providing I play whatever part He has called me to play. I've discovered that when I step out in faith, God steps in.

Our courage needs to be grounded, not in who *we* are, but in who *He* is. The Bible says that my Lord and God is a mighty warrior.

"The Lord will fight for you; you need only to be still" (Exodus 14:14).

Never forget who is with you. The strong and courageous One is living in you and fighting for you.

"No one will be able to stand against you all the days of your life. As I was with Moses, so I will be with you; I will never leave you nor forsake you" (Joshua 1:5).

Perhaps you've become discouraged. Maybe the enemy has stopped you in your tracks. Maybe you've put things on hold. Perhaps people have said that you will never complete something or achieve your goal. Perhaps you've been intimidated by someone or become afraid. Perhaps you've begun to believe it will never happen. Perhaps you're afraid of failure or rejection.

Oswald Chambers states:

"The Christian life is one of spiritual courage and determination lived out in our flesh."[33]

Courage is lived out in the flesh by:

* Getting back on that bike again after repeatedly falling off.

* Retaking that exam.

* Applying for that promotion.

* Taking that step of faith.

* Following that dream.

* Standing up to that bully.

* Trying again after repeated failures.

* Giving that person a second chance.

What does courage mean to you?

The third thing we can learn from the narrative about Joshua is that fear robs us of our courage. Joshua was fearful, and this could ultimately have robbed him of his place in the Promised Land. It's interesting to note that the day before Joshua led Israel into the first battle to take the city of Jericho, the commander of the armies of the Lord appeared before him. I don't believe he showed up just to give Joshua a battle strategy. I suspect He was there to encourage him not to be afraid, but to be strong and courageous because, as promised, God was with him.

What was Joshua fearful of?

I'm sure there were many things.

First, his inexperience in leading the people. Would they accept him as their leader and follow him into battle? Second, the Canaanites themselves, who dwelt in a seemingly impenetrable city. Perhaps he was also afraid of failure and a lack of provision. He may have had doubts about whether he was in God's will and whether God would show up. It is not unusual for us to have doubts just before we take on a fresh challenge from God.

Joshua chose to be courageous, to put fear to one side and to lead Israel into the Promised Land. He decided that the call of God was more important than the fear he was experiencing.

What are you fearful of right now?

Whatever it is, don't allow fear to drain away your courage. Don't allow people to make you fearful, because God is sovereign. Do not fear people. God has a history of dealing with difficult people. Don't be fearful of your inability to lead or of failure. Don't be fearful of lack. Don't fear the future. Don't speculate. Refuse to allow anything and anyone to rob you of your destiny in Christ.

Perhaps it's time to discover for yourself that it's OK to be a little bit afraid as you step out into all that God has for you. I'm more and more convinced that each person who has ever achieved anything significant for God has stepped out in spite of their doubts and fears. They make a choice to simply obey God, do what they're afraid to do and step out into all that He has for them.

Eleanor Roosevelt stated: "You gain strength, courage, and confidence by every experience in which you really stop to look fear in the face. You are able to say to yourself, 'I lived through this horror. I can take the next thing that comes along.' You must do the thing you think you cannot do."[34]

Every time we choose to look fear in the face we will grow in courage, confidence and faith.

You will...

Finally, I noticed this as I was reading the words God spoke to Joshua:

"Be strong and courageous because you *will*..." (Joshua 1:6, emphasis mine).

God wants to encourage you today that, in spite of your fear, your occasional moments of doubt and your lack of courage and strength, you will succeed in all that He has called and purposed you to be and do. You *will*. He is with you. His grace is sufficient for you. As Paul says:

"I can do all things through Christ who strengthens me" (Philippians 4:13, NKJV).

Father,

You know me better than I know myself. There are times when I feel weak, when I lack courage and feel afraid. Thank You that You don't call the people who have it all together. Thank You that You call the Gideons, Joshuas, Esthers and people like me.

I refuse to be *dis*couraged today. I will not be robbed of my courage or my enthusiasm for all that You've called me to be and do. I will fulfil my destiny. I declare that I can do all things through Christ who strengthens me, and that Your grace is sufficient for me, for Your power is made perfect in weakness. I choose not to let fear rule my heart but rather to look fear in the face and step into all that You have for me, for Your glory.

Amen

Further reading

Nehemiah; 1 Corinthians 16:13.

Chapter 20

BE STRONG AND COURAGEOUS... AND WORK

I'm sure many of us can remember heading home in fear and trepidation with our school reports tucked under our arms. I recall wondering what they contained, and whether the science teacher remembered that unfortunate incident back in the autumn term. I wondered whether there had been any sign of improvement in maths. For some reason, my walk home always seemed to take longer on those particular days...

My school reports often reflected the fact that I talked too much in class and could be a disruptive influence when bored, which happened to be most of the time. I would work hard at the subjects I enjoyed doing and felt fulfilled in, such as sport, English and history, but less so in those I didn't like, such as maths, physics, biology, geography and French.

I recently read the following record of David giving instructions to his son Solomon:

"David also said to Solomon his son, 'Be strong and courageous, and do the work. Do not be afraid or discouraged, for the Lord God, my God, is with you. He will not fail you or forsake you until all the work for the service of the temple of the Lord is finished'" (1 Chronicles 28:20).

Do the work!

I began to wonder why David was emphasising the fact that Solomon would need to "do the work" on the Temple. I wondered whether he sensed this would not be a priority for Solomon, which turned out to be pretty apt seeing as his own palace was almost twice the size and took twice as long to build.

Perhaps David also anticipated that attacks and discouragement would come. He knew, more than most, that when we try to build something for God the enemy will rise up and attempt to bring fear and discouragement into our lives. Maybe he also recognised the size of the task his son was to inherit, and that he would need to stick at it, particularly when things moved slowly, frustrations arose or challenges became too tough.

Frustrations and challenges

There have been many times when I've become frustrated by how slowly things have been moving or by what's happening around me. I've questioned why whatever it was I believed God had asked me to do wasn't happening or hadn't been successful in the way I had anticipated. However, I've realised as I've grown older that there are periods when I'm just a co-worker in one of God's grand schemes. My role at these times is to be faithful to what He has called me to do, no matter how challenging that is and no matter how much I'm struggling with it.

I have also started projects for God that I never got to continue with. He has had to reveal to me that just because He called me to launch something it doesn't necessarily mean I'm the one to see it through to completion. I've discovered that my gift has often been to launch, pioneer and establish a project, and that it is frequently others with different gifts that will take the project to the next level, but it took me some time to realise this.

Do as you're told, Jonah!

Jonah didn't ask for or desire the project God gave him to go to Nineveh:

> "'Go to the great city of Nineveh and preach against it, because its wickedness has come up before me'" (Jonah 1:2).

In fact, the narrative informs us that he rebelled and went in completely the opposite direction, eventually being brought back into God's will via the stomach of a large fish!

This story helped me understand that there will be times during our lives when God calls us to become involved in projects that are important to him but that don't seem important to us. I would even suggest that this includes projects for which we have no vision. Jonah certainly had no vision for Nineveh.

Feeling trapped?

You may feel trapped right now, and perhaps you're not where you anticipated you would be. You may feel frustrated and deeply unhappy with your life. You may see no future in what you're doing. You may look at others and wonder how you ended up here. God may be testing your obedience. He may be watching to see whether you will be faithful to do the work.

David forewarned Solomon that he might feel fearful and discouraged, but that he was to put in the hours. Yes, he was to keep at it and do the work. He was to complete the task God had called him to do.

There was a period in my ministry when I felt contained, trapped and deeply unhappy. I couldn't get my head around it, and I felt no desire for what I was doing. I had little or no long-term vision. Then God spoke to me very clearly and said: "Simon, my vision for your life is for you to be faithful and obedient to what I have called you to do now."

Wow! That was so good of God, and so liberating for me. I relaxed and began to be faithful and obedient to what he had called me to do until he opened new doors for me to walk through.

> "Now God has us where he wants us, with all the time in this world and the next to shower grace and kindness upon us in Christ Jesus. Saving is all his idea, and all his work. All we do is trust him enough to let him do it. It's God's gift from start to finish! We don't play the major role. If we did, we'd probably go around bragging that we'd done the whole thing! No, we neither make nor save ourselves. God does both the making and saving. He creates each of us by Christ Jesus to join him in the work he does, the good work he has gotten ready for us to do, work we had better be doing" (Ephesians 2:7-10, MSG).

Whatever you're doing today, and whatever your situation, please don't become frustrated like Jonah. Don't run away. Rather, thank God that He chose you for today, for this moment, and give it your best shot for the Master builder and Creator. It's incredible when you realise that God chose you before the beginning of time to take on this project, and at just such a time as this. Be encouraged; He believes in you! Your unique skills, abilities, personality and experiences are needed for this role. Use them well, work hard and give Him the glory!

Father,

Thank You for keeping Your hand on my life. I have to be honest and say that I'm feeling unhappy, frustrated and discouraged right now. Things haven't turned out as I anticipated, and I feel like I'm stuck. This is not where I wanted to be. Help me to recognise the calling on my life and to fulfil it. Help me to see and to be faithful and obedient to what you have called me to do now. I pray for fresh strength, energy, enthusiasm and joy as I work.

In Jesus' name,
Amen

Further reading

Jonah.

Chapter 21

NO MORE PITY PARTIES

Many people have either been furloughed or started working from home during the pandemic. I came to the conclusion several years ago that I needed to work from home at least two days a week in order to isolate myself from the noise and busyness of the church centre and office. Even more importantly, I needed to quieten myself, worship, pray, reflect, strategise, study and hear God's voice.

I assigned Tuesdays to start preparing Sunday messages for my congregation. During a particular period of my ministry I had become increasingly frustrated about some of the things that were happening. I have to admit that I lost three consecutive Tuesday mornings dwelling on my frustrations with people, the church and the lack of progress I was seeing. I remember just staring out of our bedroom window for hours, lost in a world of despondency and despair that became steadily worse with every negative thought and reflection.

Trapped in a cave, and perhaps having a similar experience, David cried out to God:

"I cry out to the Lord; I plead for the Lord's mercy. I pour out my complaints before him and tell him all my troubles. When I am overwhelmed, you alone know the way I should turn. Wherever I go, my enemies have set traps for me. I look for someone to come and help me, but no one gives me a passing thought! No one will help me; no one cares a bit what happens to me. Then I pray to you, O Lord. I say, 'You are my place of refuge. You are all I really want in life. Hear my cry, for I am very low. Rescue me from my persecutors, for they are too strong for me. Bring me out of prison so I can thank you. The godly will crowd around me, for you are good to me'" (Psalm 142:1-7, NLT).

Overwhelmed

I'm sure many of us have been there; overwhelmed by everything that is happening... or in my case, *not* happening; frustrated and disappointed by life's rich – or better, poor – tapestry; wondering how things have become so bad; sinking into a dark abyss of despair... and enjoying the pity party to end all pity parties!

You may be surprised to discover that two of the leading giants of the Old Testament, David and Elijah, were prone to the odd pity party. We mentioned earlier that Elijah, having killed all the prophets of Baal, and with his life under threat from Jezebel, ran away:

"Elijah was afraid and fled for his life. He went to Beersheba, a town in Judah, and he left his servant there. Then he went on alone into the wilderness, traveling all day. He sat down under a solitary broom tree and prayed that he might die. 'I have had enough, Lord,' he said. 'Take my life, for I am no better than my ancestors who have already died'" (1 Kings 19:3-4, NLT).

Having taken on the demonic forces at work in Israel only a few hours earlier, Elijah was became so despondent that he asked God to take his life. In the midst of his anguish, God provided food and rest, then enquired of him: "What are you doing here, Elijah?" (see 1 Kings 19:9).

What are you doing here?

In the midst of all my pity parties I have eventually found my way out of the dark place by asking myself the same question: "What are you doing here, Simon?" Sometimes it's a real challenge to escape that place of gloom and despair, and the sadness can feel overwhelming. I know... I've been there. It's not so much that you're enjoying it, but that your feelings are controlling you at this point.

However, we mustn't allow ourselves to dwell there if we can possibly help it. "How do I escape?" you ask. Rather than focus on all the negative, despairing and critical voices around me, I begin to worship and praise God, reminding myself of all that God has blessed me with, all that He is doing now and the amazing people He has placed around me. As you can imagine, the list becomes longer and longer as I begin to receive a truth-based, godly perspective on my situation.

I had to recognise that this was a ploy the enemy was using in my life at that time and refuse to allow myself to get into such a negative place. He was seeking to fill my mind with negative voices, either from within or without, in order to overwhelm and debilitate me. Those Tuesday mornings became completely unproductive and wearying, and I achieved nothing. I also realised that my Monday schedule, which was filled with meetings, often left me feeling emotionally and spiritually flat on a Tuesday. I've since addressed this. Sometimes a bit of wisdom is required.

I also had to learn how to fight back in prayer. I had to put on the whole armour of God (see Ephesians 6:10-18), and in particular the helmet of salvation. I needed to make prayerful declarations over my life that I would not allow myself to be controlled by despondency, despair and discouragement. I had to make a decision that I would no longer walk down that same street and fall into the same hole every Tuesday... or any other day, for that matter! I decided to walk down another street.

Go to God

David also found himself in the midst of an enormous pity party at Ziklag. He and his men had gone off to battle with the Philistines and had returned to discover that their camp had been raided by the Amalekites and burned to the ground. Their wives, children and possessions had been taken captive. They had lost everything, and, in their anger and devastation, David's men were ready to kill him. How did he respond?

"David was greatly distressed because the men were talking of stoning him; each one was bitter in spirit because of his sons and daughters. But David found strength in the Lord his God" (1 Samuel 30:6).

However he didn't allow himself to sink into despair. David found strength and encouragement in God when all seemed lost and his men wanted to kill him. He found a way through, and mercifully God gave him a plan, using an unexpected source (an Egyptian slave) to direct them to the Amalekite camp so everything that had been lost could be fully restored.

However bleak your situation may look right now, please look to God for encouragement and expect Him to use unexpected people and sources to provide you with direction. When you do so, he will bring breakthrough and restoration.

David's distress was a direct result of poor decision-making. What was he doing attempting a fight with the Philistines? Why did he leave his camp, which was filled with wives and children, unprotected? Sometimes we can be the creators of our own distress and discouragement.

Perhaps, on occasion, the situations we find ourselves in are a direct result of our own poor decision-making and lack of wisdom. This is not always the case of course; sometimes life just happens. Whatever circumstances you find yourself in today, and no matter how discouraged you feel, refuse, absolutely refuse, to attend your own pity party. It is a scheme the enemy will use to entrap you, paralyse your faith and destroy your belief in God.

So refuse to be discouraged today. Be expectant for God to break through, and remember this:

> "...Weeping may last through the night, but joy comes with the morning" (Psalm 30:5, NLT).

Father,

You know everything I'm facing right now. It just seems like there's so much to contend with. At times I feel anxious and overwhelmed by my thoughts. I'm wearied by everything I have to deal with in this season. However, I make a choice today: no more pity parties!

I choose not to allow myself to remain discouraged. I pray that You will strengthen me, instilling in me fresh energy, enthusiasm and courage to handle all that I'm facing today. May the joy of the Lord be my strength.

In Jesus' name,
Amen

Further reading

Ephesians 6:10-18.

Chapter 22

THE SHEEP HAVE BIG TEETH

It was a Christian prophet who gave my wife the words featured in this chapter heading when we were going through a particularly difficult time during our early years of ministry. We had faced a barrage of false accusations, lies and criticisms that weren't only untrue but were also extremely hurtful. Julia was attending a ladies' event when the prophet commenced her teaching ministry by asking Julia to stand up. She began her prophecy by stating: "You've discovered that the sheep have big teeth!" It perfectly described what we had been experiencing.

That was a horribly dark and painful season for Julia, me and our family. False accusations were made against us, so people began avoiding us and refusing to speak to us, even though we had done nothing wrong. Worse still, our young children were deeply affected. I can't remember a tougher season in our lives. We were both totally discouraged and on the verge of quitting ministry altogether. This was discouragement with a capital D.

It is tragic that so many in God's Kingdom suffer from so-called 'friendly fire'. Julia and I have seen it all too often during our time in ministry. In fact, I know of many pastors and leaders who have suffered at the hands of others, along with their families. Ministry is not for the fainthearted! Guys, pray for your pastors and leaders. Support them. Think the best of them. Encourage them. Bless them. They are not perfect. Just like you, they are learning. They often have to make incredibly difficult decisions that won't please everyone, and yes, they will also make mistakes.

Perhaps you have been facing some sheep with big teeth or a person with big teeth who is quick to bite! It's really horrible when it happens, but remember that the person attacking you is one of God's children. They may not realise the impact of their words or actions. They may feel they are acting completely righteously. Perhaps they are being used by the enemy to attack you. Maybe they are hurting because they've been hurt themselves in the past and it's the only language they understand. Start by remembering who your battle is really against:

> "For our struggle is not against flesh and blood, but against the rulers, against the authorities, against the powers of this dark world and against the spiritual forces of evil in the heavenly realms" (Ephesians 6:12).

How to respond

If you're having a tough time right now, and are feeling discouraged by the behaviour of others, remember these six things:

*   We are to love people in spite of their sinful behaviour. Sometimes, just like us, they will get things wrong and behave badly. Most of us have criticised and judged people wrongly at some point. Didn't Jesus say something about those who were entitled to throw the first stone?

- Keep a short account with God and with others. Forgive, forgive, forgive. I've discovered that making a choice to forgive in my head eventually led to a heart that was able to do the same. It starts with a choice, and God does the rest.

- Remember that you're in good company. Jesus was falsely accused. They called Him a glutton, a drunkard and a friend of sinners (see Matthew 11.19). He was despised and rejected, yet He never defended Himself. The people accused the apostle Paul of being a madman, and a babbler (see Acts 26:24 and 17:18). He was accused of being a troublemaker who stirred up riots (see Acts 24:5) The Bible calls Satan the "father of lies" (see John 8:44), and if you're committed to doing God's will he'll attack you, often using other people to do so.

- Please try not to become discouraged, and don't despair. That's hard, I know. I've been there more than once. It's a massive challenge, particularly while the battle is still raging. Ask God for grace in place of the aggression you may be feeling inside.

Remember this: the attack is a sign you're achieving something of significance or are about to have some sort of breakthrough. In my experience, the enemy doesn't waste his time with those living on easy street. He attacks those who are a threat to his kingdom.

- Accept that you may never be vindicated. I'm not sure we ever were, and it's something I stopped looking for a long time ago. I'm at peace with it. The important thing is to be keep your heart right, and to be faithful and obedient to what God has called you to do. That is victorious living. Let God deal with other people; that's His job. He knows best.

- Pray for those who oppose you. Jesus Himself taught us this:

"But I say, love your enemies! Pray for those who persecute you!" (Matthew 5:44, NLT).

So pray for them. Ask Him to fight this battle on your behalf, to soften hard hearts and to give fresh understanding to those who oppose you. Pray for relationships to be restored and for you to learn from this experience. Ask Him to bless those who persecute you. Yes, really bless them! That can be a challenge, but do it anyway.

Remember the words of James:

> "Consider it a sheer gift, friends, when tests and challenges come at you from all sides. You know that under pressure, your faith-life is forced into the open and shows its true colors. So don't try to get out of anything prematurely. Let it do its work so you become mature and well-developed, not deficient in any way" (James 1:2-4, MSG).

You know what? God considered you worthy of this challenge. Perhaps you've never seen it that way before. He believed you were more than capable of facing it and coming through it stronger. He will use this experience to teach you things you never could have learnt on easy street and that will serve you well in the future.

"Conflict is a powerful tool in the hands of God and can be used to teach a leader lessons he would not learn in any other way"[35] (J. Robert Clinton).

Looking back on the situations we've been through, I have to say that each one of them has taught us so much about ourselves and our leadership skills, and has generally reinforced our faith in God. Each one has been an invaluable vehicle for discovery and learning. I wouldn't have missed these opportunities, painful as they were at the time. We are better people and leaders for it.

Father,

I've discovered that the 'sheep' around me have big teeth at times. I'm facing a real battle right now.

Help me not to be fearful or anxious, but rather to trust deeply in You. I choose to demonstrate grace and mercy rather than judgement. I forgive all those who have opposed, judged, criticised, lied and spread false accusations about me. I choose to guard my heart and love rather than judge, and to bless rather than curse.

Father, I ask You to fight this battle on my behalf. Please intervene. Soften hearts and change attitudes, mindsets and opinions. May every plan of the enemy fail and come to nothing. Help me to really trust You in this season and to know Your peace, which passes all understanding.[36] May it fill my heart and mind as I rest in Christ Jesus. And finally, may I learn things from this situation that will strengthen my faith and make me more like Jesus.

Amen

Further reading

Micah 6:8; Philippians 2:1-11 and 4:4-9.

Chapter 23

THE HELPER IS AT HAND

J ust recently I went on my regular early morning run. I really
enjoy running and have all the gear: quality running shoes and
clothes, along with an armband to put my phone and house key
in. However, on this occasion I returned home after an hour's
run to discover that the key had somehow escaped from the zip
pocket of the armband and was nowhere to be seen. Thankfully, Julia
was at home so I could get back inside the house.

At this point I could easily have given up on my lost key, but instead
I asked God to help me find it. We went for a walk with the dog
that evening and retraced my running steps for about a tenth of the
course, but there was no sign of it. What do you do in a situation like
this? I refused to give up, and again asked God to help me find the
key. I remembered the words of Jesus that He would send the Holy
Spirit as our Helper:

> "And I will pray the Father, and He will give you another
> Helper, that He may abide with you forever – the Spirit of
> truth, whom the world cannot receive, because it neither sees
> Him nor knows Him; but you know Him, for He dwells with
> you and will be in you. I will not leave you orphans; I will come
> to you" (John 14:16-18, NKJV).

I realised it was going to be like finding a needle in a haystack, particularly seeing as the run had involved several different laps of a park with trees. However, the next time I did my run, some two days later, I asked the Helper to help me find my key. About three miles in, I exited the park and ran down a side road, and there was our house key lying in the middle of the road. Praise the Lord! I was so excited I pulled off a personal best running home to tell Julia!

The Holy Spirit – our Helper – is at hand. We only need to ask.

Daniel found himself in an impossible situation. He was in big, big trouble. He couldn't obey the king's decree that no one should pray to any god or human other than the king for the next thirty days, but he knew that anyone who did would be thrown into the lion's den (see Daniel 6:7). He simply had to honour and obey God.

I must have read the passage below so many times, but there was one thing I'd never noticed before. I knew that Daniel prayed three times each day, as was his habit; however, it was the content of his prayer on this particular day that caught my eye. He was asking God for help:

> "Now when Daniel learned that the decree had been published, he went home to his upstairs room where the windows opened towards Jerusalem. Three times a day he got down on his knees and prayed, giving thanks to his God, just as he had done before. Then these men went as a group and found Daniel praying and asking God for help" (Daniel 6:10-11).

It sounds as though he was still asking when they walked in on him. He must have been far from convinced that his prayers had been answered when that knock sounded on the door! Help hadn't arrived, trouble had... and worse was to come in the form of a den full of lions!

We know the rest of the story, of course. Daniel, in his wisdom, and knowing that the outlook was poor, had asked God for help. It wasn't immediate, but it came nevertheless when God shut the mouths of the lions. I'm not sure that has ever happened before or since, and even King Darius was happy to acknowledge God's intervention in this situation:

> "He rescues and he saves; he performs signs and wonders in the heavens and on the earth. He has rescued Daniel from the power of the lions" (Daniel 6:27).

God help us!

There is a common expression many people still use: "God help us!" Maybe if we made this our prayer more often He would! God can't answer prayers that have never been prayed. No matter whether we're in a crisis or have a run-of-the-mill need, God helps.

How often do we struggle on, become discouraged and then either try to work things out or attempt to change the situation ourselves, while God is sitting on the heavenly sidelines longing for us to utter those words "God help me!"? It delights Him when we ask for help. He loves to help His people. We simply need to ask.

My still childlike faith allows me to bring the small and the large before my Father to ask for His help. One day it might be a lost key and another some financial provision. It might be help with a project, or wisdom and insight in dealing with a difficult situation or person. Whatever it is, I know the Helper is at hand, and I'm never afraid to ask, and to keep asking, until an answer comes or breakthrough occurs.

Sometimes it's hard to pray and even harder to know *what* to pray. Thank God that His Holy Spirit is willing to step in and help us at these times as well. Paul writes:

"...The Spirit also helps our weakness; for we do not know how to pray as we should, but the Spirit Himself intercedes for *us* with groanings too deep for words; and He who searches the hearts knows what the mind of the Spirit is, because He intercedes for the saints according to *the will of* God" (Romans 8:26-27, NASB).

Ask Him to help

A practice I have adopted, which has yielded much success, and particularly at incredibly busy and stressful times, is to simply pray through the day's diary or job list and ask God for help with whatever I'm about to face. You would be amazed to hear what God has regularly done in either stretching out the time, allowing unimportant appointments to be cancelled, bringing about unexpected offers of help from other staff members or volunteers, tasks being completed more quickly than anticipated... the list goes on. Never be afraid to ask the Helper for help.

Most of us don't like asking for help (ask any woman who has been lost in a car with her husband, but the husband has refused to ask anyone for directions!). We prefer to try sorting things out for ourselves. That's crazy really, considering that we know the One who threw stars into space and who owns the cattle on a thousand hills (see Psalm 50:10). We can learn so much from God's Word, which reminds us how much He loves to help His people:

"Don't be afraid, for I am with you. Don't be discouraged, for I am your God. I will strengthen you and help you. I will hold you up with my victorious right hand" (Isaiah 41:10, NLT).

"God is our refuge and strength, an ever-present help in trouble" (Psalm 46:1).

Have you noticed that it delights God to help you? What do you need to ask Him for help with today? Don't be afraid to ask for whatever is on your heart. He is your Helper.

"The Lord is with me; he is my helper. I look in triumph on my enemies" (Psalm 118:7).

Father,

Thank You that You help me in my weakness. I come to You today to ask You to help me in [list the areas]. You are my God and my Helper. While I wait for Your assistance, help me to trust in You deeply and to remain expectant, even if things appear to get worse (as they did for Daniel) before they get better. Help me to continue to pray and trust You deeply until a breakthrough occurs. Help me to grow stronger in my faith today and every day.

In Jesus' name,
Amen

Further reading

Hebrews 4:16 and 13:6; Psalm 54:4.

Chapter 24

AS A MAN THINKS...

We live in challenging times. How do you view your life right now? Would you say your glass is half-empty or half-full? The way you respond to this age-old question may reflect your outlook on life, your attitude towards yourself, and whether you feel optimistic or pessimistic about your life.

Our thoughts shape our attitudes, actions and words. Minister and columnist Dr Frank Crane said: "Our best friends and our worst enemies are our thoughts."[37]

It's certainly true that our thoughts have incredible power over our lives.

How is your thinking today?

Perhaps you're feeling negative, discouraged or disillusioned. Perhaps nothing seems to have changed for some time and you're wondering where God is in your situation. Perhaps you don't expect or believe that anything will ever change. Perhaps this has developed into negative self-talk, complaining, criticism and envy. Perhaps you're simply worn out and feel as though you want to quit. Perhaps you're seeing others through the same negative prism with which you're viewing your own life right now.

How we think dictates who we are and how we live. It controls our attitudes, behaviours, words and actions. The way we think sets the tone in all our relationships and has the power to influence the spiritual atmosphere in our homes, schools, colleges and workplaces; in fact, anywhere we are present. The thoughts you entertain and the things you expose yourself to will shape your mind, and will eventually impact your character and destiny.

Solomon put it like this:

"For as he thinks in his heart, so *is* he..." (Proverbs 23:7, NKJV).

Change your life

In order to change your life, you must change your thinking. That will be particularly hard if you've been thinking a certain way for many years, but with God's help it can be done. The apostle Paul encourages us with these words:

"Do not conform to the pattern of this world, but be transformed by the renewing of your mind. Then you will be able to test and approve what God's will is – his good, pleasing and perfect will" (Romans 12:2).

In fact, the New Living Translation translates it like this:

"...Let God transform you into a new person by changing the way you think..."

You may feel as though you could never change the way you think right now. Perhaps you've been thinking the same things in the same ways for years. Nevertheless, Paul states that God can do it. He can transform your life by changing the way you think. Nothing is impossible for God. Why don't you give Him permission to change your thinking and transform your life today?

Ground rules

How about establishing some ground rules? I did an exercise similar to the one below in my prayer journal, where I made some promises to God and myself:

I will:

* Be shaped and influenced by the Word of God (see 2 Timothy 3:16-17), guarding my heart and mind from other worldly influences and taking care over what I watch, read and listen to.

* Choose my friends carefully, removing negative, critical and judgemental people from my inner circle (see 1 Corinthians 15:33).

* Choose to walk by faith, not by sight (see 2 Corinthians 5:7).

* Seek the mind of Christ and His thoughts (see 1 Corinthians 2:16).

* Dwell on the right things (see Philippians 4:8).

* Choose my position, being positive, faith-filled and expectant. People and situations can change in a moment with just a phone call, text or email, but I will stand firm and hold my position (see Luke 21:19 and 2 Corinthians 1:21).

* Accept that I can't always see the full picture. Only God can (see 1 Corinthians 13:12 and Isaiah 55:8-9). He knows best and His timing is perfect.

* Watch my self-talk and believe the best about myself. I am a child of God (see Ephesians 4:29 and John 1:12).

- Surprise everyone, even in the midst of discouragement and challenge, by being the most positive person in the room (see 1 Thessalonians 5:16-18).

- Lead my family well during challenging seasons (see Deuteronomy 6:6-7, Ephesians 6:4 and 1 Timothy 3:5).

I won't:

- Allow the enemy to plant negative thoughts in my head. I will resist him until He flees from me (see James 4:7).

- Dwell on the negative or allow my thinking to be viewed through a lens of discouragement (see Philippians 4:8).

- Speculate, try to work things out in my own mind, prejudge outcomes or lean on my own understanding (see Proverbs 3:5-7).

- Worry about things that aren't yet proven (see Philippians 4:6-7.

- Allow the world to shape my thinking or beliefs (Romans 12:2).

- Let others cause me to lose my peace and positive, faith-filled attitude (see Romans 16:17-18 and Titus 3:10).

What can you put in place today?

Here are some practical suggestions to help change your thinking:

- Decide which thought you need to change first (focus on one at a time).

- Choose some encouraging verses or promises from the Bible that apply to this thinking. Place them where you can regularly access and meditate on them (I put them in my iPhone notes).

- If appropriate, meditate on any prophetic words you have received in the past that have helped and encouraged you.

- Use prayer declarations. I use these a lot. I've discovered that when I pray in the Spirit my prayers often contain scriptural truths and promises. I thank God for helping me pray in this way. I will often write those prayers down and use them for a few days, declaring those truths over my life.

- Feed on God's Word, and fill your home and life with worship. The more you read His Word the more powerful and effective your prayer life will become (see point 4 as an illustration).

- Be accountable to a friend. Ask this friend to pray for and check in with you regularly.

I've found this really works. Consider what your life could be like from now on if you put these simple practices into place and were transformed by the renewing of your mind.

Father,

My mind has been a battlefield of late. I'm aware that my thinking hasn't been godly, right or true. I take captive every thought that does not conform to Christ. Please forgive me. Help me to adopt your thoughts about You, myself, others and my life.

I want my mind to be filled with the wonderful things your Word describes: faith, hope, grace, love, joy, peace, kindness and patience. I want to think about things that are true, noble, right, pure, lovely, admirable, excellent and praiseworthy. May my attitudes, behaviours and actions change as a result.

Father, thank You that Your Spirit helps me to have self-discipline and a sound mind. In fact, Your Word declares that I have the mind of Christ.[38] May my life be totally renewed by the transformation of my mind, and may those closest to me notice the difference, for Your glory and honour.

Amen

Further reading

Isaiah 55:8-9; 2 Corinthians 10:5; Philippians 4:8-9;
2 Timothy 1:7.

Chapter 25

NO MORE GOOD INTENTIONS

A few years ago I took my monthly prayer retreat to a beautiful and peaceful Anglican retreat house called Shepherds Dene in rural Northumberland. Shepherds Dene is a large old house set in woods with a river that meanders through the woodland. It is a place where God has spoken to me on many occasions.

On this particular day I was walking in the fields close to the retreat when I noticed a farmer ploughing on the other side of the valley. In an instant, God spoke to my heart and said: "Everything that farmer does is intentional, and everything I do is intentional. You need to learn to become more intentional."

God wants us to be more intentional about prayer. He longs for us to turn those good intentions to pray into actual prayer action.

"The largest pool of untapped resources in the world today is humans' good intentions that don't translate into action"[39] (Lloyd Nimetz).

Intentional praying

Let's be intentional about praying. Good intentions get us nowhere, but God moves and things change when we pray. Breakthroughs happen. Miracles occur. A divine exchange takes place. The impossible becomes the possible. The stuck become the unstuck. The imprisoned become the delivered. Bondage is broken. Strength returns. Healing occurs. Minds are renewed. Vision is restored. Joy replaces sadness. Discouragement is replaced by fresh courage. Life returns in abundance.

We have to be intentional about prayer, particularly during the most challenging seasons. There have been periods in my life when I've felt so discouraged, despondent and battle-weary that praying was the last thing I felt like doing.

On days like this it can be a real challenge to pray. We may be tempted to ask ourselves, "What's the point?", especially when nothing ever appears to change. Yet these are precisely the times we need to pray and stay especially close to God. The mistake so many Christians make when they're busy and stressed is that they spend less time with Him, but that's when we need to carve out time to really seek His face.

The truth is this: God is more than able to answer our prayers, but in order to receive an answer we must first pray:

> "Now to Him who is able to [carry out His purpose and] do superabundantly more than all that we dare ask or think [infinitely beyond our greatest prayers, hopes, or dreams], according to His power that is at work within us, to Him be the glory in the church and in Christ Jesus throughout all generations forever and ever. Amen." (Ephesians 3:20-21, AMP).

Many of the men and women in the Bible were intentional about praying. Consider Daniel, who set aside time to pray three times a day (see Daniel 6:10-11); Esther, who called the Jews to pray and fast with her for three days to save the Jewish people (see Esther 4:16); Moses, who was intentional about spending time with God in the tent of meeting outside the camp (see Exodus 33:7-11); and of course Jesus, who would rise early to pray and often withdrew to a solitary place to seek God (see Mark 1:35; Luke 5:15-16; Luke 6:12).

Can I encourage you to be more intentional about prayer? Set some time aside and find a place where you won't be disturbed as you pray. It will transform your life. I believe prayer is the most underutilised source of power in our Christian lives.

We need to rediscover the incredible power of prayer, and even more so during seasons of challenge, discouragement and attack.

We must pray when we're anxious, fearful and in need of renewed courage. As Karle Wilson Baker wrote:

Courage is Fear
That has said its prayers.[40]

Nothing you can do during those seasons will benefit you more than prayer. Nothing. It will change you spiritually, mentally and physically.

How should we pray?

We must ask the Father!

We do not have because we do not ask. People in Newcastle, where I pastored for more than ten years, had a great expression: "Shy bairns get nowt!". It meant that people shouldn't be afraid to ask for things, because if they were, they would end up with nothing.

"'So I say to you: ask and it will be given to you; seek and you will find; knock and the door will be opened to you. For everyone who asks receives; he who seeks finds; and to him who knocks, the door will be opened'" (Luke 11:9-10).

These are familiar words. We must remember that God is our generous and loving heavenly Father. Unlike our earthly fathers, He is more than able to open the storehouses of heaven. So ask Him.

We must ask in faith

Simply asking God for things won't get you a positive answer. You must ask in faith!

> "And whatever things you ask in prayer, believing, you will receive" (Matthew 21:22, NKJV).

How do we develop enough faith to see our prayers answered? By praying and seeing prayers answered! Start small. You might not have the faith to pray for someone to be healed, but you might have enough faith to pray for a small amount of money for food. We must believe when we pray that God will answer our prayers.

We must be specific

In my first book, *Imagine*, I tell the story of a time when my young daughter prayed for the exact same bicycle her friend had. We had no money to buy her a bike as Julia and I were at Bible college, but she was gifted the exact same model by a lady who knew nothing of my daughter's prayers. Incredible!

I don't believe God does vague. In fact, after years of praying specifically for things, I've seen remarkable provision, blessing and miracles in just about every context of my life. So many of those things are listed in the chapter about God's provision (see chapter entitled 'God will provide'). Praise God that He answers specific, intentional prayers.

We must put past disappointment to one side

We have all experienced times when we prayed and prayed but God didn't seem to act in the way we expected. We didn't get that job or promotion, that person we prayed for didn't get healed, that house sale fell through, or we didn't get on that course we wanted to attend.

But listen, while there may be many reasons why our prayers weren't answered as we would have liked, we must accept that He knows best. Oswald Chambers puts it like this:

"Jesus never mentioned unanswered prayer; He had the boundless certainty that prayer is always answered. Have we by the Spirit the unspeakable certainty that Jesus had about prayer, or do we think of the times when God does not seem to have answered prayer? "Every one that asketh receiveth." We say – 'But... but...' God answers prayer in the best way, not sometimes, but every time, although the immediate manifestation of the answer in the domain in which we want it may not always follow. Do we expect God to answer prayer?"[41]

So whatever your personal experiences have been, don't keep looking back. Move on, and keep praying faithfully and intentionally. Refuse to become discouraged.

We must abide in Christ

"If you remain in me and my words remain in you, ask whatever you wish, and it will be done for you" (John 15:7).

This is a very important promise. When we abide in prayer and spend time with God, fellowshipping with the Holy Spirit and listening to Him, we develop spiritually, so that His desires became ours. This results in us seeing incredible answers to prayer.

We must ask in accordance with the will of God

Knowledge of scripture is so important here. The Bible tells us about the will of God, so that when we ask for something we can know with certainty that God has promised to do it.

"This is the confidence we have in approaching God: that if we ask anything according to his will, he hears us. And if we know that he hears us – whatever we ask – we know that we have what we asked of him" (1 John 5:14-15).

We must learn to be persistent in prayer!

One of the things that I've noticed about God's people is that they tend to quit praying very quickly. We simply must learn to be tenacious in prayer; to pray and not give up (see Luke 18:1-8).

I believe that during the toughest seasons we must learn to pray persistently and to struggle, strive, wrestle, fast, plead earnestly and seek God until we experience a breakthrough. There will be seasons when we can do nothing but pray. Seasons when our faith is stretched. Seasons when, through prayer, we learn to depend on the grace of God more than ever before.

Are you praying enough?

If we're honest, many of us have pretty weak prayer lives, sometimes consisting of a quick five minutes in the shower or a passing thought in the car on the way to work. As Jesus says in Matthew 26:41: "… The spirit is willing, but the flesh is weak."

Can I challenge you to set aside time every day to pray? Find a time that suits your lifestyle, then schedule some prayer; particularly if you're in the middle of a storm right now.

If you're already praying regularly, step it up. Pray several times a day. Set a reminder on your phone. Don't worry if you feel as though you're repeating the same prayers. Ask, seek and knock (see Matthew 7:7). Persist. Keep going!

Stand on and claim the promises of God. He is faithful to *all* His promises. Don't doubt, but rather believe. Pray until something happens. And don't forget to leave time to listen to your heavenly Father. He may have a suggestion that will unlock your situation.

R.A. Torrey said:

"When the devil sees a man or woman who really believes in prayer, who knows how to pray, and who really does pray, and above all, when he sees a whole church on its face before God in prayer, he trembles as much as he ever did, for he knows that his day in that church or community is at an end."[42]

Power up your prayer today. Be intentional. Increase the regularity. Expect God to move. Anticipate and look out for signs that God is at work in your situation. Celebrate all that He is and does.

Father,

Forgive me for not regularly spending time with You in prayer. Help me to cultivate a relationship with You through Your precious Holy Spirit. Restore to me my love and passion for You, Father. I choose today to be more intentional in my prayer life and to keep praying consistently and persistently. Teach me to wrestle in prayer like Epaphras (see Colossians 4:12) until I see the breakthrough happen. Thank You that every storm will eventually pass, and in the meantime help me to stand firm, to stay strong and courageous, and to be expectant that change will come.

Amen

Further reading

Luke 11:1-13; 18:1-8.

Chapter 26

DON'T GIVE UP ON YOUR DREAMS

In 1949, Nicholas "Niki" Andreas Lauda was born into a wealthy Austrian banking and business dynasty. He soon discovered a love for motor racing, but fearing that he would bring the Laudas into disrepute, his family refused to support him financially. Niki worked hard, borrowed money and worked his way through the various levels of racing, eventually catching the attention of Ferrari. In 1975, he became Ferrari's first world champion for more than a decade.

Having won five races during the 1976 season, he was the hot favourite to win the championship again until he had a horrific accident at the German Grand Prix in Nürburgring. Niki crashed and his car burst into flames, causing him to suffer third-degree burns, several broken bones and damage to his lungs. He had lost half an ear and his face was badly disfigured. Niki's condition was so severe that a priest read him the last rites.

Sheer will power got him through, however. Refusing to give up on his dream, he was back in the Ferrari just six weeks later at the Italian Grand Prix in Monza. With blood seeping through the bandages on his head, Niki finished fourth. He came second in the championship that year, winning the title again in 1977 and, having taken a break from the sport, in 1985. After this, he went on to successfully launch his own airline, Lauda Air.

Niki Lauda is an example of someone who never gave up on his dream. In spite of all kinds of challenges, he achieved the vision he had in his heart. Not many of us are called to be motor racing champions, but we were all born for a purpose, and God has placed a calling on each of our lives.

For the most part, I have lived my life according to the vision God has given me at various points. As a teenager I dreamed of leading the camp I attended each year. As a young adult I dreamed of becoming a pastor and missionary in England. At Bible college I dreamed of planting a church in Crewe. Later, when we were in Newcastle, I dreamed of establishing a Dream Centre, where people could come and have their physical and spiritual needs met. With God's help, all these things came to pass.

During the second half of my life I've started to fulfil the dream I had as a little boy of writing books. I realised this dream with the publication of *Imagine: Trusting God Like Never Before* at fifty-four years of age.

> "Delight yourself also in the Lord, and He shall give you the desires of your heart" (Psalms 37:4, NKJV).

I believe God gives each one of us dreams and visions for our lives. Sometimes people have one dream that guides and directs their whole life, while others will have different dreams and visions for the different seasons. I love how creative God is, and how varied and exciting He allows our lives to be.

Let God lead

I believe the dreams we have are birthed from the desires He plants in our hearts, which develop into dreams we then carry. The starting point, of course, is that our lives are fully surrendered and submitted to Him. Once we have done that we can trust Him to lead us into the unique calling on our lives rather than just chasing our own fantasies.

Pastor John Hagee says:

"Sometimes you have to let go of the life you pictured, in order to have the life that God has planned."[43]

I believe this is the necessary starting point if we are to achieve anything worthwhile in life. This allows us to be led and directed by God himself, and to fulfil His plans and purposes. I've said for many years that there is a place for each one of us where we can be fulfilled *and* fulfil God's purposes for our lives. The secret is to discover that place and dwell there.

Abraham dreamed that his descendants would be as numerous as the sand on the seashore. Joseph dreamed of ruling over his brothers. Moses dreamed of the Promised Land. Nehemiah longed to see the walls of Jerusalem rebuilt.

Each of the above had to wait for their dream to be fulfilled (though Moses never actually entered the Promised Land during his time on earth because of his disobedience, only being able to view it from a distance until he entered it with Jesus at the Transfiguration). Perhaps you feel discouraged because your dream hasn't been realised as yet.

Vision awaits an appointed time

The book of Habakkuk reminds us to write our dreams (or vision) down and to be patient as we wait for God to bring them to pass:

> "And then God answered: 'Write this. Write what you see. Write it out in big block letters so that it can be read on the run. This vision-message is a witness pointing to what's coming. It aches

for the coming – it can hardly wait! And it doesn't lie. If it seems slow in coming, wait. It's on its way. It will come right on time'" (Habakkuk 2:2-3, MSG).

As I look back on my life, I realise I've discovered several things about vision:

First, vision demands patience. The phrase "Rome wasn't built in a day" is as relevant today as it ever was. Don't be discouraged if you haven't seen what you expected to have seen by now. I had to wait ten years from the time I was initially called into ministry to became a pastor, fifteen years to launch the Dream Centre and forty-eight years to publish my first book (having first dreamed about it as a child). But none of that time was wasted. Frustrating as it appears, God's timing is always perfect. He knows best.

Second, hang on to it tenaciously. If God has given you a vision it's worth clinging to with every fibre of your being. Sometimes even the people closest to us can become negative about our vision. As Joseph discovered, there may be wisdom in keeping your vision to yourself, and doing so could save a lot of heartache.

Third, don't become frustrated or discouraged, but rather use the time well. As anyone who has had a baby knows, there are many preparations to make before the joyful day arrives. The cot, pushchair, baby clothes and other equipment need to be purchased, and the nursery needs to be prepared for the new arrival. It's too late to do these things on the day of birth.

What can you do to prepare well for the moment when your dream finally comes to pass? What do you need to learn or study? What needs to change? How can you best prepare those around you? What needs to be put in place? Use the time you have now to good effect. In fact, understand this: God also needs to see that you're ready and prepared.

Fourth, if your dream is for some sort of promotion or leadership position, please don't strive. Simply allow God to open the right doors. You can't force them open yourself; He has to do it. This was a lesson I had to learn myself. When I was younger I was so ambitious and up for anything, and I felt frustrated that I wasn't able to immediately commence a role I knew God had called me to take on.

During those early years of ministry God dealt with my heart and taught me a really important principle that helped me and gave me an amazing sense of peace and security. I was reading my quiet time notes one day and the text said this:

"It is God who judges: he brings one down, he exalts another" (Psalm 75:7).

The heading was simply this: "Let God Promote You". Underneath, it said this: "If you don't find your significance and your self-worth in God, you'll spend your life trying to promote yourself."[44]

As the verse suggests, I had to come to the realisation that in God's Kingdom you don't *achieve* spiritual success, you *receive* it from God (and He's pretty astute at giving it when you're good and ready!). That day I surrendered this particular dream to God and made a commitment that I would give my all for the Kingdom, allowing God to decide the path I would take and the heights (if any) I would reach.

The postscript is this: several years later, when God felt I was ready, I took up the leadership position I believed He had given me the vision for as a teenager. God is so good!

I would encourage each one of you today, whether you find yourself in a ministry context or in secular work, to make a decision today to work hard and do your best, but not to strive. Let God promote you!

Fifth, let God work on and in you. When I was first called to ministry I served as an intern for eighteen months under a wonderful, godly Baptist minister named Rev Stuart Clarke. He took me under his wing and taught me so much. I remember him occasionally saying things like, "There are a few rough edges that need smoothing down, Simon" and "You're not the finished article yet". He was so right, and the truth is that God is still working on me to smooth off some of my rough edges today!

So don't become discouraged if your dream is taking longer than you anticipated to become a reality. Perhaps God is working on you and smoothing down some rough edges, honing and refining you, teaching you lessons He knows will be helpful in the future, and adding to your faith and experience. He is an investor in people. His desire is for His followers to be fully trained and prepared for when the vision comes to fruition. We should work with Him in this.

"This vision is for a future time. It describes the end, and it will be fulfilled. If it seems slow in coming, wait patiently, for it will surely take place. It will not be delayed" (Habakkuk 2:3, NLT).

Father,

Please forgive my frustrations. I surrender myself to You again today, and I humbly surrender the vision I believe You have given me. If it's not from You, I release it today and ask for fresh vision. If it is from You, please give me the tenacity to hold on to it, the grace to be prepared and equipped by You for it, the willingness not to strive for it and the patience to wait for it, knowing it will surely take place and will not be delayed.

Amen

Further reading

Genesis 37-45.

Chapter 27

ABOVE ALL ELSE, GUARD THE HEART

At the age of thirty-nine I decided I wasn't going to be fat and forty! I could see that I needed to lose some weight and regain my fitness. My primary motivation was to look after my heart. While nothing in life is certain, I knew I would have a better chance of leading a healthy life in my latter years if I addressed the issue during my middle years. I felt it was worth the investment.

At the point of writing this book I am fifty-six, and I've been regularly working out at the gym for the past seventeen years. In the past year I've taken up parkruns, and I now run three times a week, extending my distance to just over five miles. I believe my heart and weight are now in pretty decent shape.

Solomon gave some great advice on this front. He said:

> "Above all else, guard your heart, for everything you do flows from it" (Proverbs 4:23).

Our hearts are at the very centre of our being; the part that affects who we are; that defines our reactions, responses, actions and inactions in any given situation.

"It is the essence of who you are. It is your authentic self – the core of your being. It is where all your dreams, your desires, and your passions live. It is that part of you that connects with God and other people"[45] (Michael Hyatt).

When our children were young we had an old Toyota Space Cruiser. It was a great car: eight seats and an absolute answer to prayer when all seven of us had to travel anywhere. I still remember its massive dashboard, which I thought was so modern and high-tech at the time.

However, we had a sensitive engine warning sign that would appear from time to time, particularly when travelling long distances on family trips or holidays. It was bright red and engine-shaped, and it filled me with horror every time I saw it. Sometimes it would come on briefly and then go off, but it caused no end of panic regardless. Was there a serious problem? Were we going to arrive at our destination? Should we call the breakdown services?

Any modern car dashboard would give us an up-to-date analysis of the state of our vehicles, including engine performance, oil, water, tyre pressure, speed, fuel, air temperature and so on. It would warn us if the engine oil is running low or the engine temperature is rising.

Check your dashboard

So, how is the dashboard of your heart today? What warning lights might be flashing up? Perhaps it's a wrong attitude, unforgiveness, anger, pride, lethargy or a lack of time spent with God. Maybe your spiritual passion is waning, your peace is evaporating, your heart is becoming hard or you are experiencing a coldness in your worship. Are there any warning lights flickering away in your heart?

Can I encourage you to keep an eye on your heart's dashboard and to guard it with all diligence? It is so critical to your journey through life. It is also the place deep within; the centre of our being that responds when turbulence, pressure, trauma, problems, threats, hostility, disappointment, bad news or sickness comes along. Our hearts should influence the outer world rather than the outer world influencing us. The truth is this: if we neglect our hearts the outer will shape the inner.

Abundant life

We must make a choice to guard our hearts; not just from the challenges of life, but also in order to enjoy the abundant life we were created for in Christ. Everything we do flows from the heart, and your heart condition will overflow into your thoughts, words and actions. Health, harmony, life, peace, joy, contentment, faith, grace, mercy, goodness, enthusiasm and purpose all flow from a healthy heart. Our relationships, careers and ministries depend on it. The heart determines the course of our lives and can be a great blessing to others.

"A cheerful heart is good medicine, but a crushed spirit dries up the bones" (Proverbs 17:22).

When our hearts are right we begin to change and become the people God created us to be. When our hearts are right it impacts every sphere of our lives. So how can we guard our hearts well?

Stay connected to God

It's critical that our lives don't become so busy that we have no time for God. I'm convinced that one of the devil's ploys is to make us so busy that we will have little or no connection with God.

What are you doing to stay connected to God beyond your attendance at Sunday services? How can you become more God-conscious all day, every day? Are you starting the day well by reading His Word and spending time talking and listening to Him?

Have you considered going to bed earlier and getting up earlier to achieve this, or turning off the television and social media to spend time with God? Why not use the opportunity to pray and worship while your home is empty rather than catching up on jobs? There will always be jobs that need doing!

Listen closely to His words

I've discovered that regularly reading God's Word creates the opportunity for God to speak to me about my life, family and ministry. In Proverbs we read the following:

> "My child, pay attention to what I say. Listen to my words. Never let them get away from you. Remember them and keep them in your heart. They will give life and health to anyone who understands them. Be careful how you think; your life is shaped by your thoughts" (Proverbs 4:20-23, GNT).

God's Word still speaks:

> "For the word of God is alive and active. Sharper than any double-edged sword, it penetrates even to dividing soul and spirit, joints and marrow; it judges the thoughts and attitudes of the heart" (Hebrews 4:12).

The Word of God will help you guard your heart. Feed and nurture your heart with the Bible. Read it, meditate, consider, ask God to speak, memorise and keep it in your heart. Make a note of what you have read, then apply it.

If you're spending more time reading other matter rather than His Word, ask yourself: who is my greatest influence?

Regular check-ups

I have regular check-ups with the dentist and hygienist (although I'm not too keen on the hygienist, as she mostly tells me off for not cleaning my teeth thoroughly enough and eating too many sweets!). When was the last time you checked your heart with God? David said:

> "Search me, God, and know my heart; test me and know my anxious thoughts. See if there is any offensive way in me, and lead me in the way everlasting" (Psalm 139:23-24).

At times I have become aware that my heart wasn't right. I've realised that I had developed attitudes and responses that simply weren't normal for me and weren't good. It is so easy to allow the world, our flesh and the devil to damage our hearts. Without realising, we can become proud, cynical, judgemental, selfish, impatient, negative, discontent, envious, covetous, jealous, angry, bitter, unforgiving, fearful, resentful, unkind, impure, joyless, hard-hearted and many more things besides.

Sadly, if your heart is unhealthy this will overflow into every other area of your life, impacting your family, friends, neighbours, church, career and everything else.

Perhaps you need a heart check-up with the help of the Holy Spirit. Jesus said:

> "Blessed are the pure in heart, for they will see God" (Matthew 5:8).

I don't know about you, but I want to see and experience God more than I already do.

Refuse to be defiled by your life experiences

"Each heart knows its own bitterness, and no one else can share its joy" (Proverbs 14:10).

Life just stinks at times. We've all been on the receiving end of poor treatment from others. I've had people wish me dead, try to wipe the floor with my wife, write horrible things about me to the council, in newspapers and on social media, turn people against me, trash my character, question my motives and accuse me of things I've never done. When life happens and people sin against us, we must make a choice to guard our hearts. We must choose to protect them and refuse to harbour hurt, rejection, judgment, bitterness, anger, unforgiveness and negative thoughts. I've discovered that it's not so much that we hold on to unforgiveness and bitterness, but rather that they hold on to us. Allow God to step in and heal your damaged heart. Trust me, He is so good at doing that.

"He heals the brokenhearted and bandages their wounds" (Psalms 147:3, NLT).

Why don't you invite God in to heal your heart today?

Watch your speech

"Above all else, guard your heart, for everything you do flows from it. Keep your mouth free of perversity; keep corrupt talk far from your lips" (Proverbs 4:23-24).

Where do perverse thoughts and words come from? They come from our hearts:

"A good man brings good things out of the good stored up in his heart, and an evil man brings evil things out of the evil stored up in his heart. For the mouth speaks what the heart is full of" (Luke 6:45).

If our hearts aren't healthy they will infect others. We can so easily defile ourselves and others with our tongues. Let's make sure our hearts are right and that our speech is pure and life-giving:

"The mouth of the righteous is a fountain of life, but the mouth of the wicked conceals violence" (Proverbs 10:11).

Above all else, let me encourage you once again to:

"Keep vigilant watch over your heart; *that's* where life starts" (Proverbs 4:23, MSG).

Prayer

Father,

My heart hasn't been right of late. I ask You today, and in the days ahead, to reveal to me the true state of my heart. I long for a heart that is soft, malleable and pure; a heart that is right with You and with others; a heart after Your own heart; a heart that can be calm in the midst of the storm; a heart that determines the right course for my life; a heart that is a blessing to others. So please, Father, cleanse and purify my heart today.

Amen

Further reading

Colossians 3:12-17; Matthew 15:16-20.

Chapter 28

YOU ARE NOT A FAILURE

As you've probably realised by now, David is probably my favourite of all the Bible characters. His story is laid out before us, warts and all. He was an incredible leader and warrior; however, he wasn't infallible, and he messed up badly at times. There is hope for us all!

His most serious failing occurred when he saw a very beautiful woman named Bathsheba bathing on a nearby rooftop and sent his messengers to get her. David slept with Bathsheba and she became pregnant, but the fact she was married put David in quite a predicament. He arranged for her husband Uriah, who was a soldier, to be placed where the fighting was fiercest. David commanded the troops to withdraw at this point, causing him to be killed.

The narrative tells us how Nathan the prophet revealed David's adultery and the murder of Uriah. The Bible states:

> "...But the thing David had done displeased the Lord"
> (2 Samuel 11:27).

There have been times in my life when I know my actions have displeased the Lord, and the same will be the case for you. What do you do when you mess up? What do you when you've done something you're ashamed of; when you have a skeleton in the closet no one except you knows about; when you've failed to complete a project or quit too soon; when you've let other people down; when you have a secret sin you feel guilty and ashamed about; when you've allowed yourself to fall into sin and there appears to be no way back?

The enemy is really good at using the guilt and shame of our past failures to keep us ensnared in discouragement and condemnation. God never brings *condemnation* (that's the other fella!), but at times He will bring *conviction*, which enables Him to really work in our lives.

Psalm 51 outlines David's response to God. Why don't you pause and read it in its entirety right now?

In light of this, what should we do when we slip up?

Admit and confess our sins

"Have mercy on me, O God, according to your unfailing love; according to your great compassion blot out my transgressions. Wash away all my iniquity and cleanse me from my sin. For I know my transgressions, and my sin is always before me. Against you, you only, have I sinned and done what is evil in your sight; so you are right in your verdict and justified when you judge" (Psalm 51:1-4).

David admitted his sin to God. He was completely honest with Him, hiding nothing. We need to confess our sins to God and also sometimes to others. One of the biggest mistakes we can make is to not admit our mistakes, faults, sins and failings. There are times when we simply need to humble ourselves and hold our hands up to whoever has been impacted: spouses, children, workmates and fellow Christians. There is something powerful and liberating about confessing our sins to one another (see James 5:16).

Confession is still necessary and important to God. Some people teach that we don't need to confess our sins any more because all our sins – past, present and future – were dealt with at the cross. They would say that God's grace is enough; that it covers all our sins. Of course it does. Absolutely. However, we must be careful that such an understanding of grace doesn't create a licence to live as we please, ignoring our sins because grace already has them covered.

> "What shall we say, then? Shall we go on sinning, so that grace may increase? By no means! We are those who have died to sin; how can we live in it any longer?" (Romans 6:1-2).

It's still important and necessary to regularly confess our sins:

> "If we claim to be without sin, we deceive ourselves and the truth is not in us. If we confess our sins, he is faithful and just and will forgive us our sins and purify us from all unrighteousness. If we claim we have not sinned, we make him out to be a liar and his word is not in us" (1 John 1:8-10).

Confession causes us to:

- Remember the true sacrifice of Jesus.

- Take our sin as seriously as God does. We often treat it too lightly!

- Reflect on our lives.

- Ask God to help us stop living that way.

This is why Communion is still important. Most churches today will regularly take time to pause, reflect and remember the incredible sacrifice of Jesus on the cross with the breaking of bread and drinking of wine (or juice). This is an opportunity for us all to reflect on our lives, confess any known sin and become right with God.

Embrace brokenness rather than blaming others

"My sacrifice, O God, is a broken spirit; a broken and contrite heart you, God, will not despise" (Psalm 51:17).

David's sin broke him. He was distraught about what he had done. It broke the heart of the man after God's own heart! Our sin should concern us more than it does. God doesn't take it as lightly as we do, and it can cause Him to withdraw from or even discipline and punish us.

If our sins weren't important to God, why did Jesus have to die? My sin and yours cost Jesus His life and a horrific death on a cross.

"Sin is deep, pervasive, deceptive, seductive and powerful. It ensnares all of us, but it's no match for the liberating power of God's grace"[46] (Paul David Tripp).

David didn't blame anyone else for his actions. He recognised that he alone had sinned and fallen short of God's expectations. Then he willingly received the forgiveness God, by His incredible grace, had provided.

Receive your forgiveness

David committed two terrible sins, but he confessed them and asked God to forgive him. Later, when reflecting on this, he was able to pen the words of one of the most famous psalms ever written:

"Praise the Lord, my soul, and forget not all his benefits – who forgives all your sins and heals all your diseases, who redeems your life from the pit and crowns you with love and compassion… he does not treat us as our sins deserve or repay us according to our iniquities. For as high as the heavens are above the earth, so great is his love for those who fear him;

as far as the east is from the west, so far has he removed our transgressions from us" (Psalms 103:2-12).

Note that God completely forgave David, so why do you consider your sin, mistake or failure to be the only one God can't forgive? The Bible tells us there is no condemnation for those who are in Christ Jesus (see Romans 8:1). God forgives you, so perhaps it's time you forgave yourself for everything you still feel guilty and ashamed about from your past. Settle it in your heart today. Declare aloud right now:

"Through the finished work of the cross, I am forgiven. Jesus Christ died once and for all my sins. No further sacrifice for sin is necessary. I am free from the guilt and shame at last. I am a child of God."

And know this: God loves you and has not abandoned you. Billy Graham wrote:

"Disappointment and failure are not signs that God has forsaken you or stopped loving you. The devil wants you to believe God no longer loves you, but it isn't true. God's love for us never fails."[47]

Look ahead

God has already forgiven you, so stop looking in the rear-view mirror! Stop revisiting those skeletons, those past sins, that guilt and shame you feel. Don't allow the enemy or other people to keep using your past against you.

"'Forget the former things; do not dwell on the past. See, I am doing a new thing! Now it springs up; do you not perceive it? I am making a way in the wilderness and streams in the wasteland'" (Isaiah 43:18-19).

Don't keep going over old ground. Failing does not make you a failure! (Simon) Peter's life demonstrates to us that it's possible to fail without becoming a failure, so stop beating yourself up. Failing at something can cause massive discouragement and may cause you to describe yourself as a failure, but it's time to move forward and leave the past behind.

"Place a line of demarcation between your past and your present: 'That was then, and this is NOW!'[48] (T.D. Jakes).

Whatever you have been through or are going through, please hear what I'm about to say. Yes, you failed. Yes, you messed up. No, God has not finished with you yet. Abraham, Isaac, Jacob, David and Jonah all messed up; not forgetting Simon Peter, who denied Jesus three times yet went on to lead three thousand people to Christ on the day of Pentecost and to establish the early Church.

Failing doesn't make you a failure. It actually puts you in the company of some of the biblical greats.

So perhaps it's time to dust yourself down and, one step at a time, to move forward into all that God has for you. He loves you, accepts you, forgives you and is calling you back from that place of failure and disappointment. It's time to leave failure behind. It's time to take courage and begin to move forward again.

Father,

Thank You for speaking directly into my life today. I confess my failings before You [bring them to God now]. I receive Your mercy, forgiveness and grace. Help me to know that I am accepted and loved, and that I belong to You.

I choose today to stop going over old ground. I'm aware of my past, but I'm more excited by my future. I know you have plans and purposes for me; plans to prosper me and not to harm me; plans to give me a hope and a future.[49] Help me to stay close and in step with you today and every day.

Amen

Further reading

Ephesians 2:1-10; 1 John 1:8-9.

Chapter 29

COURAGE IN SUFFERING

A t the time of writing this, the nations of the world are facing the worst pandemic we have seen for a hundred years. COVID-19 is no respecter of persons, and there is fear and anxiety everywhere. Thousands of people have died, and many have experienced untold loss and suffering.

Life is far from easy at times, and most of us will experience suffering or trials of one kind or another at some point. As I mentioned previously, I have faced loss, financial disaster (nearly losing our home), bereavement, betrayal, rejection, attacks, loneliness, stress, anxiety, burnout and sickness. I have even reached such a point of despair that I've wondered whether things would ever change.

The Oxford English Dictionary defines suffering as: "The state of undergoing pain, distress, or hardship."[50] Suffering also involves the misery or loss resulting from affliction or misfortune.

The Bible is a fascinating narrative of people's lives. It records the many incidents of suffering individuals face: death during childbirth, rape, incest, murder, poverty, betrayal, kidnap, bereavement, loss, famine, war, persecution, stoning, martyrdom, sickness, death and barrenness.

The suffering servant

Jesus is described as the "suffering servant" (see Isaiah 53, NASB) and Paul actually boasted of his sufferings (see 2 Corinthians 11:23-30). A quick read of the latter part of Hebrews 11 informs us of the suffering and persecution experienced by the early Christians.

If you're suffering today, you're in good company. It's interesting to note that, in this generation of health and wealth teaching, the biblical viewpoint seems to suggest a different kind of world. Only a few heroes of the faith experienced victory or triumph over their circumstances, while many were persecuted for their faith, experienced severe suffering, and even, on occasion, became martyrs. However, they all demonstrated incredible God-given courage and were sustained by Him throughout these trials. Fulfilment for them came in the form of eternal glory in Christ Jesus. So the question is this: how can we be courageous during times of suffering?

Even as I write, I'm aware there will be people reading this who are living with bereavement and loss, have perhaps received a terminal diagnosis, or may be facing other devastating situations I have never faced myself. If so, my heart goes out to you. My prayers are with you. Life can be really tough at times.

Whatever your situation, please consider these three things today:

First, we're called to share in Christ's sufferings. Paul said something absolutely crazy. Steady... are you ready for this? I still can't believe he actually said this:

> "I want to know Christ – yes, to know the power of his resurrection and participation in his sufferings, becoming like him in his death, and so, somehow, attaining to the resurrection from the dead" (Philippians 3:10-11).

Paul's life had been so transformed by the love of God and His relationship with Jesus that his desire was to suffer with Christ. Nothing was too difficult for Paul. There is a sense in which, as God's children, we are also called to share in His sufferings at times.

We should never anticipate that the journey of faith will be a walk in the park. There may be a price to pay because we love Jesus Christ and are committed to following Him. In any case, disease, sickness and loss are all part of living in this sin-sick and sin-affected world. As a result of our suffering, we know we will be allowed to share in His glory, both in the here and now and in eternity.

"Now if we are children, then we are heirs – heirs of God and co-heirs with Christ, if indeed we share in his sufferings in order that we may also share in his glory. I consider that our present sufferings are not worth comparing with the glory that will be revealed in us" (Romans 8:17-18).

Second, don't forget that the same power used to deliver us also sustains us. Keep praying and believing for His deliverance and healing if that's what you need right now. He is the God of miracles, and He still works them for His glory. But He is also the God who sustains:

"Too often we marvel at the delivering power of God and overlook His keeping, strengthening and enabling power"[51] (Joyce Meyer).

The apostle Paul, who himself suffered continually with what he described as a "thorn in the flesh, a messenger of Satan, to torment him" (2 Corinthians 12:6-7) discovered this for himself. Three times he pleaded with God to remove it, and this was God's response:

"But he said to me, 'My grace is sufficient for you, for my power is made perfect in weakness.' Therefore I will boast all the more gladly about my weaknesses, so that Christ's power may rest on me'" (2 Corinthians 12:9).

Never forget that the power of God isn't only for deliverance, or that His grace is sufficient during times of suffering, difficulty, trial and temptation. He provides strength, power and courage during these times.

As I look back over my life, there have been some massively challenging and painful times when God hasn't instantly delivered me. But I can say that, without fail, He has sustained me through each and every situation I have faced. He has given me His incredible peace and the strength I needed to get up each day and go again. I can think of numerous situations when God has been my absolute rock and fortress. I would never have got through it all without His daily strength and sustenance.

Third, while God never sends these trials, He does use them for our good and for His glory. What the devil meant to cause harm and destruction, God will always work for good. I've discovered that there are several clear benefits to suffering, and that it is possible, in some ways, to embrace what you are going through and allow it to become a fruitful and productive season. Paul suggests that suffering is beneficial to us:

> "Not only so, but we also glory in our sufferings, because we know that suffering produces perseverance; perseverance, character; and character, hope. And hope does not put us to shame, because God's love has been poured out into our hearts through the Holy Spirit, who has been given to us" (Romans 5:3-5).

Suffering reinforces our faith, develops our trust and often causes us to pray more. It moulds and develops the character of Christ in us. It strengthens and prepares us for all that God has purposed and planned for us in the future. It enables us to be secure in God and also brings glory to Him. Peter sums this up well:

"Friends, when life gets really difficult, don't jump to the conclusion that God isn't on the job. Instead, be glad that you are in the very thick of what Christ experienced. This is a spiritual refining process, with glory just around the corner" (1 Peter 4:12-13, MSG).

"Character cannot be developed in ease and quiet. Only through experience of trial and suffering can the soul be strengthened, vision cleared, ambition inspired and success achieved"[52] (Helen Keller).

Can I encourage you today to be courageous in your suffering and trials? Of course, keep praying for deliverance, for healing, for a miracle and for a swift end to the problem, but also recognise that God is at work in this season, sustaining, ministering, honing, refining and equipping you:

"And the God of all grace, who called you to his eternal glory in Christ, after you have suffered a little while, will himself restore you and make you strong, firm and steadfast" (1 Peter 5:10).

Why not use the prayer below as a basis for your conversation with God?

Father,

I'm struggling right now. You know everything I'm facing. Please comfort me, strengthen me, support me and help me not to give up. Grant me fresh courage today to face everything I have to face. Fill me with Your incredible peace, Your life-giving hope and a deep trust in You. Continue to sustain me through this season of suffering.

I choose to embrace what I'm going through right now. Help me to mature, learn, develop a deeper faith, be transformed and become more like Jesus. Lord, give me patience during this trial through the abiding power of Your Holy Spirit.

I also remember and pray for all those around the world who are suffering for their faith. Some are experiencing incredible suffering right now. Some are in prison, some are being tortured, and some may never see loved ones again. They will be anxious, scared, fearful, hungry and very alone. Father, protect, comfort, provide for, help and strengthen them. May they know Your incredible peace.

Amen

Further reading

1 Peter 4:12-16; Hebrews 11.

Chapter 30

RUNNING WITH HORSES

Have you ever been seeking God for a breakthrough when the situation actually became worse? The prophet Jeremiah was involved in a fierce battle with idolaters and wicked priests. He was responding to the Lord's call to condemn Judah and to predict her downfall. He faced abuse and ridicule at every turn, and attacks from almost every side. Needless to say, he was finding his calling tough. It certainly wasn't one for the faint-hearted!

He eventually became so discouraged that he poured out his heart to God (see Jeremiah 12:1-4). However, God's response was effectively, "Hey, you think this is bad... it's going to get worse. Even your own family will betray you!"

"'If you have raced with men on foot and they have worn you out, how can you compete with horses? If you stumble in safe country, how will you manage in the thickets by the Jordan? Your relatives, members of your own family – even they have betrayed you; they have raised a loud cry against you. Do not trust them, though they speak well of you'" (Jeremiah 12:5-6).

God's response initially appears harsh. However, in the midst of Jeremiah's challenging call and circumstances, He desired the prophet to grow in faith and trust, because God knew there were larger challenges ahead. We must remember that He will use everything we experience as a growth opportunity. God desires our faith to grow stronger and deeper.

> "For this very reason, make every effort to add to your faith goodness; and to goodness, knowledge; and to knowledge, self-control; and to self-control, perseverance; and to perseverance, godliness; and to godliness, mutual affection; and to mutual affection, love. For if you possess these qualities in increasing measure, they will keep you from being ineffective and unproductive in your knowledge of our Lord Jesus Christ"
> (2 Peter 1:5-8).

I have no idea what you're facing personally right now. I'm sure some of you are facing challenges you have never faced before, problems you never anticipated would appear in your life, issues for which you feel unprepared, and situations that are stretching you further than ever before. You may well be at breaking point.

For some there will be a constant desire to quit, and the temptation to call it a day may appear really attractive. I would caution you not to, but to trust God even more deeply. Determine to keep going, with His help, and face down whatever is happening in your life right now.

Whenever I struggle with life I remind myself that Jesus is praying for me and that my faith will not fail (see Luke 22:31-32). I remind myself that the great crowd of witnesses in heaven is cheering for me:

> "Do you see what this means – all these pioneers who blazed the way, all these veterans cheering us on? It means we'd better get on with it. Strip down, start running – and never quit! (Hebrews 12:1, MSG).

Anyway, back to Jeremiah. I believe there are several lessons we can learn from this encouragement to compete with horses rather than to run with men on foot.

Life's not fair at times, but you have your own life to live and your own race to run

So run it. We're often tempted to compare our lives with those of others, and to see what God is choosing to do in their lives rather than our own. As you look around, you will see that He does what He pleases and what is right. We must choose not to be envious of others or covet what they have. We should recognise that we all have a unique call on our lives and a unique race that only we can run.

> "Therefore, since we are surrounded by such a great cloud of witnesses, let us throw off everything that hinders and the sin that so easily entangles. And let us run with perseverance the race marked out for us" (Hebrews 12:1).

Your greatest pleasure and sense of fulfilment will come from running your race well.

You have a larger capacity for faith and abundant living than you realise

One day you may well be running with horses! God has more for you than you're currently experiencing.

My youngest son was a very good young footballer. As he developed, he graduated from playing for the school team, through all the various levels, until he found himself having trials with several Premier League teams. This was quite a steep learning curve for him. Within a couple of years he had gone from racing with men to competing with horses.

God wants you to grow as a Christian. He has placed you on His personal development plan so that one day you might be able to compete with horses. We are all at different stages of our spiritual journey, and we all have different levels of faith, perseverance, resilience, trust and strength. God wants what wearies you today to be something you barely even consider in a year's time! God has more for each one of us and higher levels for us to reach if we will only trust Him.

Perhaps you had just started following your calling or dream when along came a bit of adversity, opposition and difficulty. Suddenly, after a strong start, it became hard work and massively challenging. If so, make a choice, with God's help, to be strong, resolute and courageous, then work through the challenges you face at the different stages of your journey, one by one. Be determined not to allow anyone or anything that will knock you off the path God has placed you on… and refuse to play it safe!

Adversity builds faith

Jeremiah was finding life really tough. He was clearly called and chosen by God, yet he was facing serious opposition and even threats on his own life!

There have been seasons during our ministry when we have attempted to obey God and step out into new territory, but then it seemed as though all hell had broken loose. We experienced opposition like nothing we had ever experienced before. However, we soon realised that every single challenge is an opportunity to learn and grow, to trust God more deeply, to increase our ability to resist difficulties and problems, and to enlarge our faith capacity for the future.

"Consider it pure joy, my brothers and sisters, whenever you face trials of many kinds, because you know that the testing of your faith produces perseverance. Let perseverance finish its work so that you may be mature and complete, not lacking anything" (James 1:2-4).

What is your response to trials, opposition and adversity? You will either crumble, hide and blame God, or stand firm and determine, with God's help and strength, that you will get through.

"*If* you faint in the day of adversity, your strength *is* small" (Proverbs 24:10, NKJV).

Can I encourage you today to embrace adversity, allowing it to mould you, shape you and increase your faith? Be strong and courageous, for God is with you!

Discover how to conquer weariness and exhaustion

As we read before in Jeremiah 12:5:

"If you have raced with men on foot and they have worn you out, how can you compete with horses?"

Jeremiah must have been weary and even exhausted at times. I wonder what wearies you. It could be long hours, people, repetition, routine, negativity, criticism, attack, opposition or lack of sleep. I think it helps to recognise that, no matter how hard we try to maintain a balance and look after ourselves physically, there will sometimes be periods of exhaustion and weariness, so it's important to consider how to respond during these times.

People will sometimes attack and oppose us, particularly those of us who are serving God, and that can become exhausting, so again we must learn to deal with this. Jeremiah was constantly attacked, abused and even thrown into prison. His life was under constant threat. So expect to experience criticism, negative people, rejection and betrayal. This may even come from family members on occasion. That was certainly Jeremiah's experience.

These things will occur whoever you are, and especially if you are prepared to step out into what God is calling you to do. If you are a leader, in any sphere or at any level, not everyone will like or agree with you, no matter how good you are. Settle it in your heart and, with humility and God's help, lead well. You must learn how to deal with these challenges if you want to compete with horses. You can do it!

Jesus faced opposition, and so will we. In fact, if you're doing the will of God there will always be opposition:

> "...And let us run with perseverance the race marked out for us, fixing our eyes on Jesus, the pioneer and perfecter of faith. For the joy that was set before him he endured the cross, scorning its shame, and sat down at the right hand of the throne of God. Consider him who endured such opposition from sinners, so that you will not grow weary and lose heart" (Hebrews 12:1-3).

What kept Jesus going when he was opposed, persecuted, lied about and rejected? It was the prize: the cross and our salvation. Don't allow others to weary you, but rather keep focused on the goal, your calling and the joy that lies ahead, because one day you will no longer be racing with men but competing with horses.

Father,

Thank You for calling and choosing me for such a time as this. I give You permission today to continue with Your personal development plan for my life. I recognise that I have much to learn, and my desire is to become everything You have called and purposed me to be.

Help me not to crumble in the face of adversity, but to be strong in You and in Your mighty power. May I not become weary in doing good, and may I graciously endure opposition from sinful people. Thank You that You renew my strength and help me to run the race You have given me to run without growing weary.[53] Enlarge my faith capacity so that one day I will no longer race against men but will compete with horses, for Your glory.

Amen

Further reading

Jeremiah 1:4-10 and 17-19; 1 Corinthians 3:1-2; 1 John 5:3-5.

IT'S A WRAP

It's a wrap, as they say. I've done my best to share my heart and thoughts in order to help you find courage in the midst of discouragement. I hope and pray that I've achieved that objective.

Can I encourage you to revisit some of the sections that deeply impacted you, to spend time rereading them and to talk them through with God? Allow Him to minister to your heart.

We live in challenging times. Nobody really knows what the future holds, but we are blessed to know the One who holds the future in His hands. He is the only One we can truly depend on. He rules and reigns over all the earth. Providing that we make Him Lord and Saviour, we can face tomorrow with confidence, courage, strength and renewed hope.

I'll draw my thoughts to a close with this precious promise:

> "*I would have lost heart*, unless I had believed that I would see the goodness of the Lord in the land of the living. Wait on the Lord; be of good courage, and He shall strengthen your heart; wait, I say, on the Lord!" (Psalm 27:13-14, NKJV).

Simon

DO YOU KNOW THIS GOD?

I mentioned one of the most powerful paragraphs in the Bible earlier in the book. The apostle Paul declares:

> "It's in Christ that we find out who we are and what we are living for. Long before we first heard of Christ and got our hopes up, he had his eye on us, had designs on us for glorious living, part of the overall purpose he is working out in everything and everyone" (Ephesians 1:11-12, MSG).

If this is true, our days of searching to fill that hole inside of us are over. We have found what we are looking for: a personal relationship with the creator of the universe. It is astounding to think that God saw us before we were even born; that He had His eye on us and, more than that, had an incredible plan and purpose for our lives.

Perhaps you haven't connected with God yet. If not, He wants to reveal Himself to you as your heavenly Father. He loves you. He sees you. He has a wonderful plan and purpose for your life. He is the God who brings hope, restoration, peace and healing. He is the One who restores courage to the most discouraged.

If you'd like to know Him for yourself, all you have to do is invite Him into your life. You're really just saying yes to the King of the universe. You can do that by praying this simple prayer, and I promise that He will accept you:

Father God,

I come to You today. I don't know everything about You, but I know that I need You in my life. Please forgive me for all the things I've done wrong and wipe the slate of my past clean. I need a new start today. I'm choosing to trust You, and I gladly surrender my life to You. Take me just as I am, and come and live inside me through Your Holy Spirit.

Amen

If you prayed that prayer, you have just become a Christian. Welcome to the family of God! The next thing you need to do is find a lively, Bible-believing church and start attending. Speak to the leaders and tell them what has happened. If you need help with this, please don't hesitate to contact me via the email address below and I'll help you find a good church in your area.

God bless you!

Simon

Feedback

I'd love to hear your feedback on this book or, even better, to see your review on Amazon, Goodreads or wherever you purchased it. Let's join forces to help other people leave discouragement behind.

Email

If you have any comments or suggestions, or have noticed any typos, please email me at revlawton@gmail.com

Further reading

You can read more of my thoughts at simonlawton.com

Connect

Join me on Twitter, Facebook and Instagram: simonlawton

Further help

Perhaps you have been feeling discouraged for some time and this feeling has now turned into depression.

Let me encourage you to:

- Get some help. Please speak to a family member, friend or doctor. Don't allow yourself to become isolated.

- Create new habits to help improve your mental health. Exercise, take up a new hobby, join a club or do something that you've always wanted to do.

- Start attending a good local church and join one of the home groups, where you can receive helpful pastoral care and support.

- Give the Samaritans a call on 116 123 (UK only) if you need to. They are great listeners.

Imagine

If you've enjoyed reading this book, you may also enjoy my first book, entitled *Imagine: Trusting God Like Never Before*, which is based on the powerful words of Proverbs 3:5-6. It's available from Amazon and other major online bookshops.

ENDNOTES

1   Klett, L.M., "Billy Graham on Why Temptations Become Stronger After Embracing Christianity", The Gospel Herald Ministries: gospelherald.com/articles/71399/20170919/billy-graham-why-temptations-become-stronger-embracing-christianity.htm (19 September, 2017).

2   Lincoln, A., "Collected Works of Abraham Lincoln, Volume 1": https://quod.lib.umich.edu/l/lincoln/lincoln1/1:248?rgn=div1;view=fulltext (23 January, 1841).

3   See 1 Corinthians 2:16.

4   See iconicphotos.wordpress.com/2010/07/18/the-loneliest-job.

5   Nieuwhof, C., *Didn't see it coming* (Waterbrook, 2018, p. 65).

6   Lucado, M., "I Love Christmas": maxlucado.com/listen/i-love-christmas (undated).

7   Allen, C.L., *All Things Are Possible Through Prayer* (Revell, 2016, p. 51).

8   Tutu, D., cited in D. Solomon, "The Priest": nytimes.com/2010/03/07/magazine/07fob-q4-t.html (4th March, 2010).

9   Gumbele, N., Twitter.com (31st May, 2016).

10 Maxwell, J.C., *Be A People Person: Effective Leadership Through Effective Relationships* (David C. Cook, 2013, p. 164).

11 Willis, D., "7 Things your kids will remember about you": churchleaders.com/pastors/pastor-articles/307728-7-things-kids-will-remember.html (7th February, 2019).

12 Swindoll, C.R., "Attitude": store.insight.org/p-1389-attitudes-quote-color-print.aspx (undated).

13 collinsdictionary.com/dictionary/english/joy.

14 theopedia.com/joy.

15 Warren K., *Choose Joy Because Happiness Isn't Enough* (Revell, 2012, p. 31).

16 Nouwen, H.J.M., *The Return of the Prodigal Son: A Story of Homecoming* (Darton, Longman & Todd, 1994, p. 107-8).

17 See Psalm 51:12.

18 Vallotton, K., *Spirit Wars: Winning the Invisible Battle Against Sin and the Enemy* (Chosen Books, 2012, p. 50).

19 Twain, M., *The Tragedy of Pudd'nhead Wilson* (ReadHowYouWant, 2008).

20 Franklin, J., *Fear Fighters: How to Live with Confidence in a World Driven by Fear* (Charisma House, 2009, p. 58).

21 See John 10:10.

22 See 2 Timothy 1:7.

23 biblehub.com/str/hebrew/6040.htm.

24 Wiersbe, W.W., *The Bumps Are What You Climb On* (Revell, 2006, p. 13).

25 Duewel, W., cited in E. and L. Harvey, *Kneeling We Triumph* (Moody Press, 1974, p. 44).

26 Cowman, L.B.E., *Springs in the Valley* (Zondervan, 1939, p. 196-97).

27   Unger, M. and White W., Jr., *Nelson's Expository Dictionary of the Old Testament* (Thomas Nelson, 1980, p. 333).

28   Cummings, E.E., *A Miscellany Revised* (October House, 1965, p. 363).

29   lexico.com/definition/cynic

30   merriam-webster.com/dictionary/cynical?utm_campaign=sd&utm_medium=serp&utm_source=jsonld

31   The Franklin Institute, "Edison's Lightbulb": fi.edu/history-resources/edisons-lightbulb (undated).

32   Maxwell, J., "Today's Statement of Strength": johnmaxwellteam.com/2020-courage (undated).

33   Chambers, O., "Taking Possession of Our Own Soul": utmost.org/taking-possession-of-our-own-soul (undated).

34   Roosevelt, E., cited in Maxwell, J.C., *The 21 Indispensable Qualities of Leadership* (Thomas Nelson, 1999, p. 42).

35   Clinton, J.R., *The Making of a Leader: Recognizing the Lessons and Stages of Leadership Development* (essentialleadershipapps.com/uploads/5/8/4/4/58449207/the_making_of_a_leader_-_robert_clinton.pdf, p. 7).

36   See Philippians 4:7.

37   Crane, F., "Change Your Thinking": ucb.co.uk/word-for-today/9219 (12th October, 2017).

38   See 1 Corinthians 2:16.

39   Nimetz, L., "Information Overload, Action Deficit": ssir.org/articles/entry/information_overload_action_deficit (13th June, 2010).

40   Baker, K.W., "Courage": poetryfoundation.org/poetrymagazine/browse?contentId=15329 (written October 1921).

41   Chambers, O., *My Utmost for His Highest* (Marshall, Morgan & Scott, 1927, pg. 105).

42   Torrey, R.A., *The Power of Prayer and the Prayer of Power* (Aneko Press, 2020, p. 6-7).

43   Hagee, J., Twitter.com (28th April, 2016)."

44   Author unknown, *UCB Word for Today* (9th June, 1999).

45   Hyatt, M., "3 Reasons Why You Must Guard Your Heart": michaelhyatt.com/three-reasons-why-you-must-guard-your-heart (16th May, 2011).

46   Tripp, P.D., Twitter.com (27th October, 2017).

47   Graham, B., Twitter.com (21st April, 2020).

48   Jakes, T.D., tdjministries-blog.tumblr.com (4th July, 2012).

49   See Jeremiah 29:11.

50   lexico.com/definition/suffering.

51   Meyer, J., "Why Do Christians Suffer?": joycemeyer.org/everydayanswers/ea-teachings/why-do-christians-suffer (undated).

52   Keller, H., cited in *The Leadership Secrets of Billy Graham* (Zondervan, 2008, p. 177).

53   See Isaiah 40:29-31.